Get Thee behind Me, Satan:
Rejecting Evil

Fr. Kevin E. Mackin, OFM

WESTBOW
PRESS®
A DIVISION OF THOMAS NELSON
& ZONDERVAN

WestBow Press books may be ordered through booksellers or by contacting:

WestBow Press
A Division of Thomas Nelson & Zondervan
1663 Liberty Drive
Bloomington, IN 47403
www.westbowpress.com
1 (866) 928-1240

Because of the dynamic nature of the Internet, any web addresses or
links contained in this book may have changed since publication and
may no longer be valid. The views expressed in this work are solely those
of the author and do not necessarily reflect the views of the publisher,
and the publisher hereby disclaims any responsibility for them.

Any people depicted in stock imagery provided by Getty Images are
models, and such images are being used for illustrative purposes only.
Certain stock imagery © Getty Images.

Scripture texts, prefaces, introductions, footnotes and cross
references used in this work are taken from the New American
Bible, revised edition © 2010, 1991, 1986, 1970 Confraternity
of Christian Doctrine, Inc., Washington, DC

ISBN: 978-1-9736-6992-0 (sc)
ISBN: 978-1-9736-6993-7 (e)

Library of Congress Control Number: 2019910165

Print information available on the last page.

WestBow Press rev. date: 07/19/2019

CONTENTS

INTRODUCTION

On a hot, humid August day in 1960, I arrived in Washington, DC, to begin graduate theological studies. My twenty-plus classmates and I would reside and take classes at Holy Name College in the northeast section of the capital city and receive sacred theology degrees from nearby Catholic University of America.

Little did I know then that the 1960s would be a decade of incredible change in the United States and in the Catholic Church.

The presidential campaign kicked off on Labor Day, with Senator John F. Kennedy challenging Vice President Richard Nixon. After a cliffhanger election night, Kennedy became the thirty-fifth president. "Camelot" began on a cold, snowy inauguration day: January 20, 1961.

Kennedy was a Catholic and the youngest president ever elected, so we were excited. Some of us went to the US Capitol to hear his stirring inaugural address: "Ask not what your country can do for you—ask what you can do ..." We enjoyed the parade with its pageantry. It was truly a time of new beginnings. We felt the torch had been passed to a new generation, and we were that generation.

In his farewell speech, outgoing President Dwight Eisenhower had warned the nation against a growing "military-industrial complex." Some listeners were surprised that an old soldier would "bite the hand that fed him." But that warning did foretell things to come.

While we students had our daily rhythm of prayer and study, dramatic changes were percolating all around. Pope John XXIII convened the Second Vatican Council in October 1962 to reform the Church Universal. The death of "good Pope John" just eight months later brought the election of Pope Paul VI.

Meantime, new nations were proclaimed in Africa, Asia, and the Caribbean. The Cuban missile crisis shook the world. The civil rights movement gained momentum and came to a crescendo with Rev. Martin Luther King Jr.'s "I have a dream" speech at the Lincoln Memorial in August 1963. Hundreds of thousands of demonstrators demanded the passage of civil rights legislation.

And then, on November 22, 1963, President Kennedy was assassinated. I was in class when the news broke. It was as if the world stood still. Many of us watched the funeral procession on Pennsylvania Avenue, with six great horses pulling the caisson bearing Kennedy's casket slowly pacing toward St. Matthew's Cathedral. It was a somber day for all.

The 1960s could be characterized as the best of times and the worst of times—years of challenge and dissent and change. Pope Paul VI successfully concluded the Second Vatican Council with major church reforms. Newly sworn President Lyndon Johnson signed the Civil Rights Act of 1964. He also began to widen the "no-win" war in

Vietnam, and I remember the protests. Later, Rev. King was assassinated in Memphis, and Robert Kennedy was assassinated in Los Angeles.

In the middle of this turbulent decade, the pope's apostolic delegate to the United States, Egidio Vagnozzi, ordained us to the ministerial priesthood. Enroute, we also received minor orders, including the order of exorcist. My introduction to that actually occurred soon after I arrived in Washington, when I heard about a Jesuit priest who performed an exorcism in nearby Mount Rainier, Maryland.

While we as seminarians did not "do" exorcisms—as one might do medical clinical experience—the devil and demonology were very much part of Catholic tradition. We studied major sources, especially sacred scripture, thoroughly, from the beginning—the story of Genesis, noting chapter 3.

A seductive voice, opposed to God, tempted our first parents, who ate the symbolic forbidden fruit. That act of disobedience, the author wrote, explained why bad things happen (even to good people). That disobedience was seen by St. Augustine of Hippo as the fall from grace—original sin. And that explains why there's evil.

The church saw in the voice a fallen angel, called Satan or the devil. Satan and his cohort irrevocably rejected God. Satan, according to the Letter of John, is "a liar and the father of lies."

Yes, I still believe that Satan and his demons roam about this world, wreaking havoc wherever they can. They are powerful, but not all-powerful. They are creatures—pure spirits, but still creatures. It's a mystery to me that

God should permit diabolical activity, but "We know that all things work for good for those who love God" (Romans 8:28).

Before his arrest and trial, Jesus prayed for God to watch out for us, knowing we are in harm's way: "I am not asking you to take them out of the world, but that you keep them from the evil one" (John 17:15). In this petition, Satan, the evil one, the angel who opposes God, is a person. Through Satan, sin and death entered into the world, and by his definitive defeat all creation will be "freed from the corruption of sin and death" (Eucharistic Prayer IV).

In the Our Father we pray: "Deliver us from evil." When we ask that, we pray to be freed from all evils, of which Satan is the author or instigator. Evil—the devil, Satan—is real. But who is he? How does he fit into our Christian life and salvation? There's much to explore.

CHAPTER 1

THE POWER OF THE DEVIL

I canonically became an exorcist when I received minor orders at the Shrine of the Immaculate Conception in late 1961, at the hands of then Washington auxiliary bishop Philip Hannan, who later was made archbishop of New Orleans.

The Reverend Walter Schmitz, SS, master of ceremonies, orchestrated these orders like a master drill sergeant. More than a hundred of us soon-to-be-priests received the orders of porter (its symbol, keys), lector (the Bible), exorcist (laying on of hands), and acolyte (candle and cruets). In 1972, Pope Paul VI renamed these centuries-old minor orders "ministries," only retaining lector and acolyte for roles in liturgy. Major orders were reduced to two: deacon and priest. Subdeacon was eliminated.

I remember asking a classmate beforehand, what is an exorcist? He presumed, in so many words, that it's the power to call upon the name of Jesus over those who are seemingly possessed. My classmate went on to say that he heard about a youngster in his Mount Rainier, Maryland, parish who was possessed by the devil and then freed by a Jesuit priest who performed a rite of exorcism. We decided to check this out.

Sure enough, a *Washington Post* article recounted how a fourteen-year-old boy in a suburb of Washington, DC, had appeared to be possessed. The priest apparently performed the rite of exorcism a number of times. Repeatedly, each time, the child would break into a tantrum of screams, profanities, and Latin phrases—a language he never studied—when the priest intoned: "In the name of the Father, the Son and the Holy Ghost, I cast (the devil) out." Reportedly, in one of the sessions, the boy saw a vision of St. Michael casting out the devil.

William Peter Blatty, an alumnus of Georgetown University in Washington, heard about this and adapted the story for his novel *The Exorcist* (Harper & Row, 1971). The novel detailed the demonic possession of a fictional twelve-year-old girl, and two priests who attempted to exorcise the demon. In some ways the novel was a milestone in horror fiction, and it sold more than thirteen million copies.

The book's story began in Iraq, where an elderly Jesuit conducts an archaeological dig. He discovers a small statue of an ancient demon and experiences a series of omens alerting him to a pending confrontation with a powerful evil. Meanwhile, a young girl, Regan, is living with her mother, who is in the Georgetown neighborhood to film a movie. Regan becomes inexplicably ill. She undergoes troubling psychological and physical changes, refuses to eat or sleep, and becomes aggressive and violent.

After psychiatric and medical treatments, and as Regan's personality becomes increasingly distressed, her mother, an atheist, turns to local priest Fr. Karras, a psychiatrist, who discerns that Regan is possessed. He asks the bishop for permission to perform an exorcism.

The bishop designates the more mature Fr. Merrin to perform the exorcism; Fr. Karras is allowed to assist. In the middle of a series of rites, Fr. Merrin dies. Fr. Karras is left to complete the exorcism. He offers himself instead of the child. The demon seizes the opportunity to possess the priest. Karras surrenders his life by jumping out of a window and falling to his death, regaining faith in God as he receives the last rites of the church.

This horror novel, an immediate bestseller, was adapted by Blatty for a 1973 film directed by William Friedkin. The movie version, starring Linda Blair, broke box office records at many theaters and earned Blatty an Academy Award. This was also the first horror movie nominated for best picture, and the special effects made the film one of the best in its genre.

Despite many interpretations and hysterical reactions, Blatty and the novel and film assured the reader and viewer that there is a God and that this universe will have a happy ending.

The Exorcist succeeded Roman Polanski's 1968 film *Rosemary's Baby*, based on Ira Levin's novel (Random House, 1967) about modern-day witches and demons.

This psychological horror classic chronicled a fictional young couple, Rosemary (Mia Farrow) and Guy (John Cassavetes), who move into a Manhattan apartment building. Minnie (Ruth Gordon) and Roman (Sidney Blackmer) befriend them.

On the night Rosemary and Guy plan to conceive a child, Rosemary has a trance-like vision in which a demonic presence rapes her. Rosemary learns she's pregnant and suspects that she's living among a coven of witches. Meantime, her husband gets a great role on Broadway, due to another actor's sudden disability.

Eventually, Rosemary goes into labor at home and faints, and when she awakens, she's told the baby has died, which she refuses to believe.

She discovers in the next-door apartment that the coven is in full celebration. Her baby, in a bassinette with an upside-down crucifix, has the eyes of the demon Rosemary thought she imagined. The aghast young mother is told she should be honored to be the mother of Satan's son. The movie ends with Rosemary going to the cradle and gently rocking it, with a smile.

Following these blockbusters, a string of other films about the occult, Satan, and black magic appeared, including an extended "director's cut" of *The Exorcist* in 2000.

William Friedkin recently returned to the subject with his documentary *The Devil and Fr. Amorth*. Friedkin interviewed Vatican exorcist Fr. Gabriele Amorth, who worried that "Satan rules the world." The priest let Friedkin film an actual exorcism rite. "It was a harrowing experience," Friedkin testified.

When Friedkin took the footage to neurosurgeons and psychiatrists, one challenged it, saying the subject lacked "classic symptoms" of possession, such as the head turning 360 degrees and the body levitating. Friedkin informed the psychiatrist that Blatty "invented" those images. Fr. Amorth, who died in 2016, did encounter extraordinary occurrences, including dramatic personality, vocal, and language changes—but no levitation or head spinning.

So what is the phenomenon? The word *occult*, from the Latin word *occultus*, meaning hidden, secret, sinister, dark, or mysterious, can be applied generally to extrasensory experiences and para-phenomena. Kurt Koch, a theologian internationally known for his study of the subject, summarizes occultism under four areas.

1. Superstition. One example would be the number thirteen; due to a phobia shared by many people, hotels often do not mark a thirteenth floor. Another sign of "bad luck" would be a black cat walking across one's path.
2. Fortune-telling. Horoscopes, palmistry, astrology, and reading tea leaves are examples. Former first lady Nancy Reagan frequently sought the advice

of an astrologer after the attempt on President Ronald Reagan's life in 1981.

3. Magic. This appears in many guises. The most popular is probably healing magic (sometimes using an object), or alternately casting spells or curses upon someone.

4. Spiritism. This comes in many forms: Ouija boards, trances, levitations, and more.

"Deliverance" usually references freeing someone from a satanic spirit.

What, then, is a demon? The word comes from a Greek word, *dia* or *daiomai*, which means "to divide, to tear."

Demons have strong connections with animism. Animists believe that souls or spirits possess phenomena in nature (e.g., waterfalls, the sun, the moon) and that these spirits are either good or evil. Sacrifices are made to placate those they regard as evil. This understanding has given rise to various forms: for example, voodoo, practiced by some in African-Caribbean cultures as a religion.

In the Hebrew Bible we find a clear distinction between the angels of God and the fallen angels, both of which are understood to be spiritual beings. Generally, demons don't play a major role in these chapters.

In the New Testament, the noun *demon* occurs in the Gospel according to Matthew: "The demons pleaded with [Jesus], 'If you drive us out, send us into the herd of swine'" (Matthew 8:31).

The adjective *demoniac* occurs more than fifty times in the Gospels. The New Testament describes the war between the kingdom of God and the kingdom of Satan.

In 1 Peter 5:8 we find: "Your opponent the devil is prowling around like a roaring lion looking for (someone) to devour."

Jesus entered human history and thereby conquered the powers of the devil.

The problem of the demoniac—someone possessed— has weaved in and out of the history of Catholic Christianity. The medieval cults of Satan and black masses are evidence of this. Even in the twenty-first century, the question of the demoniac continues to raise its ugly head.

Psychiatrists today generally look upon someone who talks about demons as "old-fashioned." So-called possession, for many psychiatrists, is a form of mental illness. In any case, it's classified as a "dissociative identity disorder (a.k.a. "multiple personalities")—demonic possession."

In Catholic Christianity one of the symptoms of possession is described as an aversion toward the things of God. This aversion to God is a common symptom, an indication that demonic possession is not primarily a disease of the mind. It is rather the influence, and sometimes even the indwelling, of evil spirits and powers. Therefore, some argue, it seems beyond the competence of psychiatry.

So the question remains: Are there various symptoms of "demon" possession? Some argue yes: for example, a change in voice, clairvoyance, speaking in a foreign language never learned, and the deliverance from demonic possession through a healing prayer.

Though many today dismiss demonic possession as a symptom treatable by psychiatry, I would argue that there are demonically possessed people.

But we shouldn't be afraid. Jesus promised to be with

us to the end of the age. He has given us authority to cast out demons and, importantly, the example to resist their influences.

Any such contemporary discussion would include Malachi Martin's classic book *Hostage to the Devil: The Possession and Exorcism of Five Contemporary Americans* (New York: Reader's Digest, 1976). Martin is a former Jesuit, with a PhD in archaeology, oriental history, and Semitic languages.

Hostage to the Devil reads like a horror story. It's a scary and chilling book—the first I ever read where I felt uneasy and questioned whether I should stop reading it. The book explored five firsthand accounts of demon possession and exorcisms. All of the possessed were involved in sinful lifestyles, and Martin describes them graphically.

Gestures such as sprinkling the possessed with holy water and holding up a crucifix are powerful weapons against demons, Martin wrote. He tells us which prayers were used to provoke the demon and explains how exorcisms lasted rarely less than one day, and at times up to five days.

This, of course, does not jive with what Jesus did. Never do we see Jesus using objects or taking several days or using special prayers. Time and again, Jesus instructs the demons to depart, and they do.

Martin made some good points: for example, making sure you are right with God before even thinking about conducting an exorcism. He also retraced the possessed persons' lives and showed how personal choices snowballed to demonic possession. By the time a person realized what was going on, it was too late.

I found Martin's chapter "A Brief Handbook of Exorcism" especially illuminating. It described the general stages of an exorcism as presence, pretense, break-point, voice, clash, and expulsion.

First, there's an awareness of an alien or foreign presence.

Second, the evil spirit appears to be one and the same personality as the victim. The task of the exorcist is to break that pretense, to force the spirit to reveal itself openly as separate from the possessed and to name itself. Every exorcist reportedly learns that he's dealing with some force or power that is at times intensely cunning, sometimes supremely intelligent, and at other times senseless.

Third, there's the break-point: the moment when the pretense has collapsed.

The voice of the possessed is then no longer used by the demonic spirit. The sound is often unlike any human sound. The exorcist must challenge the spirit to silence and then to identify itself intelligibly.

Usually at this point, and as the voice dies out, there is the clash: the singular battle of wills between exorcist and evil spirit.

Finally, the expulsion. The evil spirit, having found a home with a consenting host, does not give up its place easily. It fights and deceives and even risks killing its host before it will be expelled. How violent the struggle depends on many things; the intelligence of the spirit being dealt with and the degree of possession are but two. The exorcist calls on the evil spirit to desist and to leave.

While some exorcists have indicated that people are possessed to some extent with their own consent,

Martin made no attempt to answer the ultimate puzzle: Why does this person rather than that person become the object of diabolic attack that can become a partial or perfect possession? The book concluded with a "Manual of Possession" and "The Roman Ritual of Exorcism."

CHAPTER 2

EXORCISMS IN CATHOLIC CHRISTIANITY

To understand the recent resurgence of interest in exorcisms, let's sketch the history of the Catholic rite.

Francis Young, PhD, of the Catholic Record Society, in his book *A History of Exorcism in Catholic Christianity* explores the shifting boundaries between church-authorized rites of exorcism and unauthorized "magic rites," from the time of Augustine of Hippo in the fifth century to Pope Francis in the twenty-first.

What precisely is a rite of exorcism? Is it a liturgical ritual, or is it simply the use of sacramental objects, such as relics or holy water, to drive out the devil and his demons from someone deemed possessed.

Exorcism often appeared as part of the liturgy of baptism in the early Middle Ages. These liturgical exorcisms continued but gradually included other methods, for example calling upon the charismatic power of a saint.

Liturgical exorcisms today, resembling the rite seen

in the 1973 film *The Exorcist*, go back to the sixteenth century Catholic Reformation. Some consider the sixteenth and seventeenth centuries the golden age of liturgical exorcisms. In the early eighteenth century, the Congregation of the Holy Office (now the Congregation for the Doctrine of the Faith) began cracking down on unauthorized manuals of exorcism. The official rite was published in 1614. Celebrity exorcists often performed their own version of the rite. Probably for this reason, the Congregation banned all manuals other than the official 1614 "Rituale Romanum," which was only replaced in 1999.

The eighteenth century saw a decline in exorcisms vis-à-vis the Enlightenment. Exorcisms still were performed in missionary territories. I remember well how Fr. Lawrence Bultmann, OFM, a Franciscan missionary, would later mesmerize novices with stories of demonic possession in Shashi, China. But generally, the decline in exorcisms continued as secular governments including France challenged such rites.

Then Pope Pius IX reemphasized the rite. Pope Leo XIII in 1893 added his "Exorcism against Satan and the apostate Angels" to the 1614 "Rituale Romanum," and included the "Prayer to St. Michael the Archangel" in the prayers after Mass. That prayer, still recited today in many churches, visualized a cosmic battle between Michael and Satan.

In the twentieth century, the novel and movie prompted by a real-life exorcism, along with a demand for exorcists, skyrocketed at precisely the moment Pope Paul VI downgraded exorcism to a remotely possible service and abolished the minor order of exorcist. In 1999 Pope John Paul II created a new rite. The founding of the International Association of Exorcists in 1994 and the publication of training courses for priests as exorcists also reinforced interest.

Pope Benedict XVI and Pope Francis both have contributed to the revival of the ministry of exorcist.

Surely a novel and movie—while capitalizing on the great conflict, Jesus versus Satan, from the greatest story ever told, the Bible—do not adequately explain the contemporary interest in evil possession. For many people today, exorcism seems like a medieval relic whose exercise is bizarre.

Interest has seemed to thrive when three factors were in play: divisiveness in the church and/or society, fear of an external spiritual enemy, and a sense of the imminent end of the world. The obsession with witchcraft also contributed to the revival of exorcisms.

And if the sixteenth and seventeenth centuries were the golden age of the demoniac, Francis Young notes, our time is the golden age of the exorcist.

Dr. Young's research approaches exorcisms as "an aspect of Catholic religious behavior, concentrating on the development of theological, liturgical and legal foundations of exorcism rather than the physical phenomena of possession."

In contemporary Catholic Christianity, exorcists confront the devil with the authority of God, and with the authority of the church, received by an explicit license from a diocesan bishop.

The literature on Catholic exorcism over the past one

hundred years can be sorted into three broad categories. The first consists of theological reflections by liturgists. The second is collections of exorcism narratives and personal testimonies of exorcists. The third category consists of critical studies from the perspective of religious history. These categories do not include the vast popular literature on exorcism and demonology.

Historical interest in exorcism focused on certain periods of Christian history. For instance, the first, second, and third centuries received a great deal of attention from biblical and patristic scholars, but the period between the fourth and tenth centuries was generally neglected, except where exorcism was treated as one form of miraculous healing among others.

Contemporary historical study of exorcism appears to be rooted in the linkage between exorcisms, eschatology and the drive to eliminate witchcraft. However the majority of studies of early modern exorcisms has focused on possession and demoniacs.

Despite the small number of documented twentieth century exorcisms, Pope John Paul II and Pope Benedict XVI fostered a revival of studies on the devil.

Demonology may not involve an exorcism and possession does not always result in an exorcism. However, there is no exorcism without possession, and demonology, to a greater or lesser extent, underlies every exorcism.

Though it is not easy to describe these three terms, the New Catholic Encyclopedia describes an exorcism as "the act of driving out or warding off demons or evil spirits from persons, places, or things that are, or are believed to be, possessed or infested by them or liable to become instruments of their malice" (1967 edition, volume 5, pages 551–53).

Whereas theologians argue that exorcism is a manifestation of God's grace, entrusted to the church and performed through the exorcist, many anthropologists view exorcisms, Christian or otherwise, as magical practices. Although the official statements of the church say that an exorcism has nothing to do with magic, it does not change the fact that rites of exorcism share similar structural features with ritual magic.

This is complicated by the fact that church exorcists might act like magicians and might introduce elements into the rite that do not have official approval.

If defined more broadly as exorcisms practiced by Catholics, the term would include the phenomena of exorcisms by means of objects, unauthorized exorcisms by clergy, lay exorcisms, baptismal exorcisms, and exorcisms that form part of magical rituals. Throughout history, laypeople have attempted exorcisms, consciously invoking church power and making use of objects believed to be imbued with sacred power, such as relics and sacramentals.

Christian exorcism is founded on an underlying belief in the power of an omnipotent God. It involves a direct imperative to spiritual beings other than God, saints, and angels. The Latin word *exorcizo* means to "swear an oath." In late Latin it came to have the sense of "to implore." The medieval Latin *coniuro* means "conjure" (raise, summon) and to conjure is an activity of the magician and exorcist alike.

Possession meant bodily possession of a human body by an evil spirit. Christians argued that the religious identity of the exorcist, rather than his or her skill, was the determining factor in the exorcism's success.

The debate about the relationship between possession and mental illness and the appropriateness of an exorcism has been replaced in the twenty-first century by new concerns. A gap remains between clergy and laity, many of whom are more concerned about haunted houses and witchcraft than with demonic possession.

The Second Vatican Council in the 1960s marked a dramatic shift in the church's engagement with society. The council rejected much of the political rhetoric of Pope Pius IX, endorsed religious liberty, and disavowed anti-Semitic or anti-Jewish statements. In the aftermath of the council, Catholic approaches to exorcism developed in line with different reactions to the council.

For some, the trend to explore more closely the liberalizing presence of Jesus and the strengths of the laity was an indication that certain church features should be downgraded or discarded altogether.

Others reacted in the opposite direction, with renewed emphasis on traditional Catholic practices: for example, exorcism. Charismatics revived a deliverance ministry, that is, "prayer of liberation" from the devil or evil spirits. In many parts of today's world, possession and exorcism have always been part of Catholic life. Exorcism was never mentioned during the council sessions. Demonology was minimized, and the devil was no more than a symbol of evil. Exorcisms became nothing more than a prayer to God to restrain the power of demons.

The minor order of exorcist was abolished in 1972.

The following statement from the Congregation for Divine Worship in 1975 summarizes the attitude:

> The special ministry of the exorcist, though not totally abolished, has in our time been reduced to a remotely possible service which may be rendered only at the request of the Bishop; in fact, there is now no right for the conferring of this ministry. Such an attitude to exorcism evidently does not mean that priests no longer have the power to exorcise or that they may no longer use it. Since, however, the Church no longer makes exorcism a special ministry, it no longer attributes to exorcisms the important role they had in the early centuries of the church.

The council's emphasis on a return to scriptural sources precipitated the reform of the exorcism rite in baptism. The downgrading of references to the devil in the revised Rite of Christian Initiation had the effect of minimizing the dramatic traditional exorcisms. In the 1960s and early 1970s, exorcisms were rare. Belief in demonic possession seemed to be disappearing because Satan himself seemed to be disappearing from Catholic belief statements. Literal belief in the devil was a relic that the church had outgrown, so many thought.

Blatty's novel and film revived thought of the possibility of demonic possession (and therefore exorcisms) among Catholics and non-Catholics. Added to this was the appearance of satanist groups.

Martin's widely read *Hostage to the Devil*, in 1976, describing exorcisms in a way that made Blatty's book seem credible, added to the revival. And with heightened popular interest, Martin initiated a process in which sacramental-style exorcism became an industry without any formal connection to the Catholic Church.

In the revised code of Canon Law, Canon 1172 reads as follows: "No one can perform exorcisms legitimately upon the possessed unless he has obtained special and express permission from the local ordinary. The local ordinary is to give this permission only to a presbyter who has piety, knowledge, prudence and integrity of life."

Fr. Amorth's 1990 book *An Exorcist Tells His Story* interestingly emphasizes the evil of witchcraft—that is, invoking a power other than God to do harm. He defined witchcraft as the worship of Satan and called such practitioners witches and satanists.

Perhaps that explains the emergence of sacramental exorcisms and charismatic evangelical deliverance ministries as a phenomenon in the last decades of the twentieth century. Fr. Amorth's book sold out twelve Italian editions before it was translated into English in 1999: the same year the first edition of the church's revised rite of exorcism appeared.

The Praenotanda to the revised rite of 1999 defined the minister of exorcism as "sacerdos" (priest) rather than "presbyter" (bishop). It insists that a priest must have special preparation and should usually be appointed by a diocesan bishop and exercise the ministry under his direction.

The introduction of this revised rite explains the origin of evil and the nature of evil spirits:

> Christ, by the Paschal mystery of his death and resurrection, has torn us from the servitude of the devil and of sin, overthrowing their rule and freeing all things from evil contagions. But when the harmful and contrary action of the devil affects persons, beings, places, and appears in a diverse way, the Church, always conscious that 'the days are evil,' prayed and prays that men might be delivered from the deceits of the devil.

The introduction makes specific reference to the danger of mistaking mental illness for possession. The exorcist is warned against exorcising those who believe themselves to be bewitched. Symptoms of possession are noted: the ability to understand languages unknown to the demoniac, knowing secrets or things happening far away, unnatural strength, and an aversion to sacred things.

The outline of the rite is: a prayer, sprinkling of holy water on the demoniac, the litany of the saints, Psalm 90, renewal of baptismal promises, the image of the cross, the threefold adjuration of Satan, an alternative formula, and the Magnificat.

The 1999 rite of exorcism was published as *De Exorcismis et Supplicationibus Quibusdam* or *Of Exorcisms and certain Supplications.* (See comparison of the 1614 and 1999 rites.)

Since Amorth's documentary book, exorcisms experienced an impressive revival. Demand for exorcism in the twenty-first century has been such that in 2005, a university in Rome began to offer a course for diocesan exorcists. Pope Francis has proved strongly supportive of exorcisms. The Congregation of the Clergy approved the International Association of Exorcists as a pontifical entity, and the United States Conference of Catholic Bishops adopted an English translation of the rite in 2014 for approval by the Congregation for Divine Worship.

Many believe the devil and his activity is real, and therefore exorcism remains a viable remedy. The exorcists, it seems, are here to stay.

Comparison of parts of 1614 and 1999 rites
1614 RR   DESQ 1999

885: O God, to whom it is proper always to have mercy and spare us, receive our prayer, so that the pity of your loving kindness may mercifully release this your servant whom the shackles of sins have bound.

47: O God, to whom it is proper always to have mercy and spare us, receive our prayer, so that the pity of your loving kindness may mercifully release this your servant Name, whom the shackles of diabolical power bind.

911: Psalm 90

50: Psalm 90

909: Nicene Creed

55: Nicene Creed

894: Behold the cross of the Lord: flee, hostile powers.

58: Behold the cross of the Lord: flee, hostile powers.

898: O God the creator and defender of the human race, who have made man in your own image, regard this your servant …

61: O God the creator and defender of the human race, regard this your servant Name, whom you have made man in your own image …

900: I adjure you, ancient serpent, by the judge of the living and the dead … I adjure you again, not by my infirmity …

62: … I adjure you, Satan, enemy of human salvation … I adjure you, Satan, prince of this world …

901: I adjure you, therefore, worthless dragon …

I adjure you, Satan, deceiver of the human race …

901: Draw back now from man, therefore, having been adjured in the name of him who formed him …

Draw back, therefore, Satan, in the name of the Father, and of the Son, and of the Holy Spirit …

903: God of heaven, God of earth …

896: I exorcise you, most unclean spirit …

81, 82, 84 (alt. formula): God of heaven, God of earth … exorcisms

904: Go out, therefore, impious one … give place to the Holy Spirit …

896: I exorcise you, most unclean spirit …

63: Magnificat

901: Therefore I adjure you, worthless dragon …

907: Magnificat

CHAPTER 3

UNDERSTANDING BIBLICAL SOURCES

The word *gospel* comes from the Anglo-Saxon word *godspell*, meaning good story/good tale. It is a transliteration of the Greek word *evangelion*, which signifies good news in a specific sense, namely the good news of a victory over an enemy.

In the New Testament this can be described as the glad tidings of salvation revealed in Jesus Christ, which introduces the new finale in the history of the world. The Gospels are summaries of this good news. Jesus is the fulfillment of prophecy. God had promised to redeem his people—the people of God—and fulfilled this promise through Jesus Christ. Yes, the good news is Jesus himself.

The Gospels are a short record of the preaching and teaching of the infant church about Jesus Christ—its Lord and Master. Matthew, Mark, Luke, and John wanted to record and summarize as faithfully as possible the fact that Christ brought, and they were handing on, the good news.

Although the Gospels give us information about the life of Christ, they are not scientific biographies. They tell the story. We have many words of Jesus. We have many facts, but not scientifically presented, for there is no scientific biography on which to base them. When was Jesus born? When did he die? We're not sure.

Though the Gospels are not a complete study, and not strictly chronological, they give us facts about Jesus. John tells us this:

> Jesus did many other signs in the presence of [his] disciples that are not written in this book. But these are written that you may [come to] believe that Jesus is the Messiah, the Son of God, and that through this belief you may have life in his name. (John 20:30–31)

The written Gospels date from about 60 AD to 100 AD between the life of Jesus (the good news) and the Gospels (the record of the good news). In between was a period in which the message of salvation was preached by scores of people throughout Asia Minor and Europe.

We can perceive three stages in the development of the Gospels. The first stage was approximately from Pentecost to 50 AD, during the verbal spreading of the good news—Jesus Christ. From about 50 AD to 65 AD there was an attempt to write down this apostolic preaching. Luke alludes to this:

> Since many have undertaken to compile a narrative of the events that have been fulfilled among us, just as those who were eyewitnesses from the beginning

> and ministers of the word have handed
> them down to us, I too have decided, after
> investigating everything accurately anew,
> to write it down in an orderly sequence.
> (Luke 1:1–3)

Long before the evangelists finally wrote the Gospels, many people attempted to make note of Jesus's accomplishments. These attempts were used by the evangelists. Matthew, for example, probably used such a document or documents for the Sermon on the Mount. Many of Jesus's sayings were gathered together and put into this one sermon.

From about 65 AD to 100 AD, the four evangelists carried forth the work and set down in writing the record of the good news.

Many factors went into the molding of these Gospels. To begin with, there was the kerygma: technically speaking the public proclamation of Christianity to the non-Christian world. Especially characteristic is its proposal of Christ and his work of salvation to the non-Christian world for the first time. It is a public and solemn proclamation of salvation accomplished through the life, passion, death, and resurrection of Jesus Christ.

The *didache*, or instruction, likewise shaped the Gospels to an extent. The kerygma implanted faith in the unbeliever. The objective of the didache was the further faith instruction of the Christian. Most of the letters as well as sections of the Gospels are didactic.

It was necessary to justify the passion and death of Jesus and to give some account of his claims to be the

Messiah—especially a suffering Messiah. The Jews were looking for a mighty king, and it was hard for them to accept a suffering Christ. The evangelist had to show why the early Christians, for example, refused to keep the Sabbath, the food laws, and so on. Their basic argument, of course, was what Jesus did and said.

The liturgical life of the church also had to be defended. Why, for example, was baptism necessary for salvation? The practice of the church is the command of Christ and hence to quote the church is to quote Christ. For example, Matthew 28:19: "Go, therefore, and make disciples of all nations, baptizing them in the name of the Father, and of the Son, and of the holy Spirit" is a reflection of the liturgy of the church. The liturgy is a result of the command of Christ.

The social conditions of primitive Christianity also helped to form the Gospels. Many problems arose in the new community in connection with their common life, and these problems led to the need for action and decision. There were people of different races, different social conditions, slaves, freed men, and patricians. The mingling of these very diverse elements led to new challenges over time.

Gentiles as well as Jews were admitted, and the question arose as to how far the Jewish law was binding upon them as Christians.

In the settling of any questions, they would inquire whether the Lord had given any pronouncement. Thus, we have the "pronouncement stories" with a minimum of detail, self-contained, with a saying of Christ.

The Gospels, in short, are a record of preaching. There

are stories and anecdotes that are to the point. There are appeals to authority that are brief. They are alive, not bookish or boring. They are the living word of God and the very preaching of the infant church.

Jesus revealed himself during his public ministry as "a man commended to you by God with mighty deeds, wonders, and signs, which God worked through him in your midst" (Acts 2:22). By his death and resurrection, he showed that he was indeed the Son of God:

> What God promised our ancestors he has brought to fulfillment for us (their) children, by raising up Jesus, as it is written in the second psalm, "You are my son; this day I have begotten you." (Acts 13:32–33)

One Gospel that enjoys preeminence is that of Mark. By calling his story "the gospel" or "good news" of Jesus Christ the son of God (Mark 1:1), Mark tells us how he planned his book. He wanted to tell his readers about the victory Jesus won, and his earthly life, by his death and resurrection, and how in the process he discloses his divine mission and person.

Mark 1:1–13 presents John the Baptist's message as the link between the utterances of the latter prophets (Mark 1:2–3) and the Gospel of Jesus. Jesus's Galilean ministry (1:14 to 9:1) serves to point up the various facets of the person of Jesus. Throughout this narrative, Mark seems to be asking readers: Who, then, is this?

Mark continually directs attention to the divine person and the mission of Jesus. Jesus himself points to it by the circumstances of his cure of the paralytic (Mark 2:1–12). He announces it unmistakably by asserting his power over the Sabbath and illustrates it dramatically by demonstrating his control of nature in the storm on the lake (Mark 4:39).

At Caesarea Philippi, Peter speaks in the name of Jesus's followers: "You are the Messiah" (Mark 8:29).

After this remarkable pronouncement, which is the high point of the Galilean ministry, the second major section of the Gospel begins. Jesus tells his followers that his life is to end with his death and resurrection and "the Son of Man must suffer greatly and be rejected by the elders, the chief priests, and the scribes, and be killed, and rise after three days" (Mark 8:31).

Jesus is then transfigured before Peter, James, and John. This only leaves them wondering what "rising from the dead" meant (Mark 9:2–10).

The scene shifts to Jerusalem where Jesus is acclaimed as the Messiah in Mark 11:1–11. He describes the future coming in power of God's dominion in the world in Mark 13:1–37. Then he inaugurates the New Covenant at the Last Supper in Mark 14:24.

All this is simply an introduction to Jesus's death and resurrection. In his trial, Jesus declares who he is, and, "They all condemned him as deserving to die. Some began to spit on him. They blindfolded him and struck him and said to him, 'Prophesy!' And the guards greeted him with blows" (Mark 14:64–65).

But upon witnessing the manner of his death on Calvary, the pagan centurion is moved to make an avowal that, in the light of the resurrection, will become the formula of Christian faith: "Truly this man was the Son of God!" (Mark 15:39).

Mark's Gospel raises many questions about the origin of the tradition and its evolution within the first Christian communities of Syria and Greece. Think about with what objective the first churches retold stories about Jesus—passed them from mouth to mouth as independent narratives or copied them from papyrus to papyrus. In the same manner we must examine the sayings of Jesus and ask with what intention these churches collected them, learned them by heart, and wrote them down.

By an analysis of the literary forms in the Gospels, Rudolf Bultmann, a German theologian in the mid-twentieth century, sought to trace the history, the needs, the aims, and the beliefs of the primitive Christian community. This analysis brings the Christian only to the early church and its creations, not to the historical Jesus. Yet, as Bultmann writes, "Indeed we can appreciate his significance only when we cease to worry about such questions."

The early Christian communities called for a common store of wisdom upon which to draw in times of crisis. Jesus is reported to have taught this wisdom. Similarly, the community desired knowledge of its future existence, and the prophetic sayings of Jesus answered questions about the time to come. Again, because the primitive church needed laws, they appeared in certain legislative forms attributed to Jesus.

Bultmann viewed the Gospels in two general groupings: the words of Christ and the narrative sections. The words of Christ are further classified as apothegm and logia. The apothegm is a little story, the center of which contains a saying of Jesus. The logia are the sapiential portrayals of Jesus as the new Moses and teacher of wisdom (for example Matthew 11:25–30), the prophetic predictions (for example John 13:36–38), and the eschatology of Christ (for example Matthew 24 and Mark 13), and the legislative, in which Jesus is the divine lawgiver (Matthew 9:3–12).

The narrative sections include the miracle stories of Jesus's ministry. The remainder of the Gospel themes include the infancy narratives, Jesus's temptation, his baptism, incidents of his public ministry, his passion, and resurrection and ascension.

One of the essential elements of this Gospel tradition is the miracle stories.

Ordinarily one thinks of a miracle as something that happens contrary to nature. In the Bible, though, a miracle means something where nature furnishes the stage for the major work of God. This takes place in the realm of history: the arena where God intervenes specifically from time to time, pressing his demands. It is these extraordinary interventions that properly speaking are the miracles of the Bible.

That there is no distinctive word for miracle is clear from a survey of the biblical words used for miracles. The miracle stories do seem to have a common form. There is a presentation of a patient to Jesus and the description, then the healing is recorded, and finally the reaction of the onlookers is described.

Mark 3:1–6 is a good example. Jesus "entered the synagogue. There was a man there who had a withered hand. They watched him closely to see if he would cure him on the Sabbath so that they might accuse him. He said to the man with the withered hand, 'Come up here before us.' Then he said to them, 'Is it lawful to do good on the sabbath rather than to do evil, to save life rather than to destroy it?' But they remained silent." Then the cure is performed: "Looking around at them with anger and grieved at their hardness of heart, he said to the man, 'Stretch out your hand.' He stretched it out and his hand was restored." And finally, there is the reaction of people to the cure by Jesus: "The Pharisees went out and immediately took counsel with the Herodians against him to put him to death."

There are general categories of miracle stories: healings, nature miracles, resurrection stories, and exorcisms.

CHAPTER 4

A BIBLICAL UNDERSTANDING
OF SATAN

In the Gospel according to Mark, Jesus cast Satan out of a man in the synagogue, as well as from a Gerasene, a Greek Syrophoenecian woman, and a boy with a demon.

Who is this Satan?

The Hebrew root from which the name Satan derives means primarily "obstruct," "oppose."

Satan does not appear in the Hebrew bible as a distinct figure responsible for all evil. While the name is applied in three passages to a being (Job 1:6–12, Job 2:1–7, 1 Chronicles 21:1), it is simply a name, defining the role that the being in question has in a particular situation. And Zechariah 3:1–2 refers to an "adversary."

First Chronicles 21:1 notes: "A Satan rose up against Israel, and he incited David to take a census of Israel." In postexile times, the concept of Satan evolved from a good angel who does God's will by policing the earth and reporting offenses to God, into a bad angel who tempts people not merely by testing them but by luring them into sin. Later the Satan whom we know to be the devil—hostile to God and mankind—emerged.

In the New Testament, Satan is mentioned by name thirty-four times. He also appears thirty-six times as "the devil."

He is likewise styled "the adversary," "the tempter," "the evil one," "the accuser," "the enemy," "the prince of devils," "the prince of this world," and "the prince of the power of the air." In 2 Corinthians 6:15, Satan bears the name of Beliar, and on other occasions he is styled as Beelzebul (Matthew 10:25, 12:24, 27; Mark 3:22; Luke 11:15–19).

Thus, Satan is an essential feature of the Gospels, integral to the narrative of Jesus. The New Testament articulates the characteristic features of Satan and his angels. John reports Jesus explaining to people, "He was a murderer from the beginning (that is, he lured our first parents into sin and thereby brought death upon all men and women) and does not stand in truth, because there is no truth in him. When he tells a lie, he speaks in character, because he is a liar and the father of lies" (John 8:44).

Jesus clarifies our choice: "Whoever belongs to God hears the words of God" (John 8:47).

Satan's power is derived ultimately from humans themselves. This is indicated by more than one New Testament writer: men and women themselves are responsible for Satan's power over them.

The idea appears clearly in Paul's letters. Human anger, for example, leaves "room for the devil" (Ephesians 4:27). He is "the god of this age" (2 Corinthians 4:4) not by right, but because people have made him so.

Satan's kingdom is diametrically opposed to God's. It includes not only the demons, but sinners, for "Whoever sins belongs to the devil, because the devil has sinned from the beginning. Indeed, the Son of God was revealed to destroy the works of the devil. No one who is begotten by God commits sin ... In this way, the children of God and the children of the devil are made plain" (1 John 3:8–10).

Satan is primarily a tempter. For example, St. Paul

explains, "Do not deprive each other, except perhaps by mutual consent for a time, to be free for prayer, but then return to one another, so that Satan may not tempt you through your lack of self-control" (1 Corinthians 7:5). Paul also gives good advice in his letters to the Galatians (6:1) and the Thessalonians (1:3:5).

Satan is able to exercise power through temptation. That was his approach to Jesus, but he failed to tempt Jesus and had no power over him.

The kingdom of Satan was established with the fall of the first humans. The earth became Satan's, and he could give the kingdoms of this world to whomever he wanted. Satan's words at the very outset of Jesus's ministry indicate this:

> Then the devil took him up to a very high mountain and showed him all the kingdoms of the world in their magnificence, and he said to him, "All these I shall give to you, if you will prostrate yourself and worship me." (Matthew 4:8–10)

> Then he took him up and showed him all the kingdoms of the world in a single instant. The devil said to him, "I shall give to you all this power and their glory; for it has been handed over to me, and I may give it to whomever I wish. All this will be yours, if you worship me." (Luke 4:5–7)

Jesus refused the devil. Each refusal is expressed in language taken from the book of Deuteronomy. This victory was begun with Jesus's coming on earth and his death on the cross and his resurrection from the dead and will reach its completion in the last days: "Therefore, rejoice, you heavens, and you who dwell in them. But woe to you, earth and sea, for the Devil has come down to you in great fury, for he knows he has but a short time" (Revelation 12:12).

Yes, Satan is the great adversary of God and of God's beloved humanity.

In the parable of the sower (Matthew 13:1–23), Satan is the evil one who comes to steal away what was sown in someone's heart. In the parable of the weeds (Matthew 13:24–30), Satan is the enemy who sows weeds or evil among people and thus creates the conflict between God's kingdom and Satan's kingdom.

St. John in the book of Revelation describes the origin of this age-old conflict: the heavenly battle between Michael and Satan, together with his wicked angels. Satan and his followers were cast from heaven because of their sin of pride and disobedience, and they were thrust down into hell, "For if God did not spare the angels when they sinned but condemned them to the chains of Tartarus (a term indicating the infernal regions) and handed them over to be kept for judgment ... then the Lord knows how to rescue the devout from trial and to keep the unrighteous under punishment." (2 Peter 2:4–9).

Because of original sin, Satan and his angels possess with God's permissive will a certain power over the world and human beings. Peter counsels in his letter:

> Be sober and vigilant. Your opponent the
> devil is prowling around like a roaring
> lion looking for [someone] to devour.
> Resist him, steadfast in faith, knowing
> that your fellow believers throughout the
> world undergo the same sufferings. The
> God of all grace who called you to his
> eternal glory through Christ will himself
> restore, confirm, strengthen, and establish
> you after you have suffered a little.

Satan and his cohorts exist by influencing the world
and humankind in every sector at all levels, making them
instruments and bearers of their power. Nothing on earth
is absolutely immune. Until the end of time, humans must
contend with this. The hope in this battle rests in Christ
Jesus, who overcame these powers on the cross and in the
resurrection. Their power was thereby drawn into the love
of the obedient son of God. At the end of time, Satan's
power will be destroyed once and for all.

The Exorcisms

The kingdom of God/kingdom of Satan conflict is
especially manifest in the Gospel exorcisms, from a Greek
word *exorkismos*, meaning to call up under oath or drive
out (an evil spirit).

The Gospels frequently mention people possessed by
the devil: having an evil spirit or under the power of such a
spirit. This evil spirit sometimes gives them a superhuman

strength. At other times, the evil spirit maltreats them and makes them act like wild animals.

On occasion, many devils took possession of a person. Seven demons had possessed Mary Magdalene (Luke 8:2); a legion took possession of the Gerasene (Mark 5:9).

The Gospels hold many references to Christ's power over evil spirits and His freeing of people possessed by demons. For example, Matthew 4:24, 8:16; Mark 1:32–34, 39; Luke 4:41, 8:2.

By a mere command Jesus casts out devils. The Pharisees accused Jesus of casting out demons in the name of Beelzebul, the prince of demons (Matthew 9:34, 12:27) and of being possessed himself (John 7:20, 8:48–52). But Christ pointed out how absurd this charge was. "How can Satan drive out Satan? If a kingdom is divided against itself, that kingdom cannot stand." (Mark 3:23–30).

It is clear that the evangelists record a large number of cases of diabolical possession in the Gospels because of their significance in salvation history. Jesus himself emphasizes this in the Beelzebul passage (Mark 3:22–26). In refuting, for example, the charge that he has power to expel devils because of a pact he made with Satan, Jesus declares that the devils are organized into a kingdom in order to attack and overthrow, if possible, the kingdom of God.

Christ is stronger than "the strong man, fully armed" (Luke 11:17–26), and he will bring to an end the kingdom of Satan.

Thus, the exorcisms inaugurate the triumph of Christ over Satan.

The Gospels preserve for us five detailed accounts of demonic possession and the cures by Jesus.

Note the way Christ deals with them. Earlier thinking looked upon those with evil spirits as especially sinful people who, through their sins, had sold themselves to the devil. For Christ, though, demonic possession did not mean a sinful person or a league with Satan, but a bondage to Satan. From the viewpoint of Christ, Satan can possess a person even against that person's wishes. So out of compassion, Christ heals these people.

Mark's opening miracle is the demoniac in the synagogue, followed by Simon's mother-in-law, and the curing of many who were sick of various diseases and the driving out of many demons the same evening.

This first set of miracles follows almost immediately the baptism of Jesus (Mark 1:9–11) and the temptation in the desert (Mark 1:12–13). The message: "This is the time of fulfillment. The kingdom of God is at hand. Repent, and believe in the gospel" (Mark 1:14–15).

The temptation was written as a unit with the baptism. It is a natural consequence of baptism and the reception of the spirit to be tested.

Mark seems to use the term "desert" primarily in a theological sense. In the Old Testament, the desert or wilderness was thought of as an uninhabited place, a place of testing. Deuteronomy 8:2 reads: "Remember how for forty years now the Lord, your God, has directed all your journeying in the wilderness, so as to test you by affliction, to know what was in your heart: to keep his commandments, or not."

The desert was also a place of blessings. Deuteronomy

2:7 declares: "The Lord, your God, has blessed you in all your undertakings; he has been concerned about your journey through this vast wilderness. It is now forty years that he has been with you, and you have never been in want."

In Mark 1:4–5, 9 we see that Jesus was already in the desert. Mark conveys that Jesus is being tested and blessed. To tempt, in the Old Testament, denotes a test of fidelity. In this context it means the same thing; Jesus is tested concerning his mission. The word also implies a solicitation to evil by the devil.

Jesus is given his mission, and his main adversary appears.

In the literature of Jewish tradition, beasts were associated with devils. The "wild beasts" are included as a parallel to the angels: evoking the image of Satan and the beasts against God and his angels. It tells us that Jesus's ministry is to be a conflict between God and Satan.

Mark's Gospel appears to place the temptation in the beginning of Jesus's ministry to show us that the Christ-Satan confrontation is to be the pattern of his whole ministry.

Thus, in the temptation, Jesus wins the first round against the powers of evil. In the power of the Spirit and in the strength of this first victory, he goes forth to proclaim the coming of God's kingdom and the overthrow of Satan's.

Perhaps this is why the first miracle in Mark is an exorcism.

Fr. Kevin E. Mackin, OFM

The Demoniac in the Synagogue (Mark 1:22–28)

All the elements of a popular story are here. First, circumstances are described: the teaching in the synagogue and the demon who perceives and resents the healer. "What have you to do with us, Jesus of Nazareth? Have you come to destroy us? I know who you are—the Holy One of God!"

The striking feature is the way in which the demon addresses Jesus. The demon, of the supernatural world, perceives Jesus to be the Holy One of God who had come to destroy the kingdom of evil.

The exorcism in the synagogue emphasizes Jesus's encounter with the demon, who proclaims his messiahship.

Then the healing is recorded: "Jesus rebuked him and said, 'Quiet! Come out of him!' The unclean spirit convulsed him and with a loud cry came out of him."

Finally, the impression produced on the onlookers is described: "All were amazed and asked one another, 'What is this? A new teaching with authority. He commands even the unclean spirits and they obey him.'"

Capernaum in verse 21 is one of the rare place names in Mark (probably on the northwest shore of Lake Galilee), and the town is mentioned in all four Gospels.

There in the synagogue where the people gathered for worship, Jesus probably spoke of the kingdom of God and the destruction of evil powers. The voice of prophecy, long silent in Israel, suddenly is heard again in the person of Jesus.

In verse 23 the demoniac interrupts Jesus and asserts: "Have you come to destroy us?" The destruction of evil powers was to be part and parcel of the messianic age. The demons know well why Jesus has come. He has come to bring in the kingdom of God and drive out the kingdom of Satan. And so, the demon asks: "What have you to do with us, Jesus of Nazareth? Have you come to destroy us? I know who you are—the Holy One of God!"

The driving out of the demons was to be the announcement of Jesus that the kingdom of God was at hand. In verse 25 Jesus rebukes the unclean spirit and charges it to be silent and come out of the possessed man. Jesus heals not with an act or a touch, but with a word. His word is effective.

This verse raises the question of the messianic secret. In Mark especially, Jesus is presented as rejecting the title of Messiah and forbidding those whom he cured miraculously from publicizing the cures.

Anyone who accepts the honesty of the evangelists can easily deduce from Mark that the reason Jesus did not wish in the beginning to be openly proclaimed as the Messiah was to avoid wild expectations of a merely political messiah. He stressed the spiritual nature of his mission, and he refused any clear title until his entry into Jerusalem on Palm Sunday.

The description of the exorcism follows in verse 26. The unclean spirit convulses the man and, crying with a loud voice, comes out of him.

As often happens in miracle stories, the reaction of the bystanders is described, in verse 27. They are astonished that Jesus casts out the unclean spirit with a word and that he teaches with such authority.

The effect is further described in verse 28 by a reference to the spread of the good news.

Mark's main intent here is to suggest the deep impression made by Jesus upon the people.

The power of Jesus over devils is a sign that the kingdom of God has come.

The Gerasene Demoniac (Mark 5:1–20)

This miracle story, set on the eastern shore of Lake Galilee, describes in detail the patient and his illness and his meeting with Jesus: "When he got out of the boat, at once a man from the tombs who had an unclean spirit met him. The man had been dwelling among the tombs, and no one could restrain him any longer, even with a chain. In fact, he had frequently been bound with shackles and chains, but the chains had been pulled apart by him and the shackles smashed, and no one was strong enough to subdue him. Night and day among the tombs and on the hillsides, he was always crying out and bruising himself with stones."

The result of the cure is narrated in the portrayal of the former demoniac "sitting there clothed and in his right mind," and is further emphasized by the man's request to accompany Jesus, and by the command to tell his friends the great things the Lord had done for him and how he had mercy on him. The man became an evangelist. "And all were amazed." (Mark 5:20)

Vincent Taylor made a series of experiments to show the tendencies of oral transmission.

Longer miracle stories, in general, stand close to the

accounts of eyewitnesses, and shorter stories have passed through many before they were written.

This enables us to group together such narratives as this and the lad with a demon in Mark 9:14–29.

Apart from the transitional phrases in verses 1 and 8, the Gerasene story appears in an original form.

Another feature of the narrative is the arrangement of scenes, shifting from the man to the herd of swine, then to the townspeople, and finally back to the man. This does not seem to be a literary embellishment; the story is what it is.

The many details, the dialogue, the expulsion, the description of the man in his right mind, the attitude of the spectators, and the kind of message the man proclaims in the Decapolis all ring true.

In verse 1, Mark describes the place of landing in vague terms. The meeting with the demoniac takes place apparently soon after. It is not necessary to seek significance in the association of the demoniac with the tombs; it was a popular belief that cemeteries were haunted by demons.

The condition of the demoniac explains easily why he lived in seclusion. His life is described in verse 5. He was crying out and cutting himself with stones.

In verse 7, he calls Christ "the Son of the most high God." Here the expression means a creature of God's special choice. Hence it does not express divinity but indicates Jesus's close relationship with God.

Verse 8 is Mark's explanation of the demoniac's frenzied words. The question in verse 9, "What is your name?" is connected with the ancient belief that knowledge of a name carries power (over an adversary and over a demon).

The name "legion" probably meant that the possessed man felt himself a collection of uncoordinated impulses and evil forces.

Verse 13 gives four details: Jesus permits the spirits to go out of the demoniac; they went out; they entered into the swine; and the swine ran into the lake.

Many critics have held that the exorcism set the herd in motion; the man hurled himself upon the swine and struck terror into them, driving them down the incline.

The swineherds flee in verse 14 and tell the townspeople what happened. In verse 15, the people come to Jesus and see the man, in his right mind.

Yet the tale of the swine convinced the people that Jesus was a public danger. Hence, they ask that he leave.

The story ends with the Gerasene man telling of the work of Jesus. Christ concretely has overcome the power of Satan.

The Woman of Canaan (Mark 7:24–30)

This is often classed as a story about Jesus rather than a pronouncement story.

The interest seems to be in the incident itself rather than in the words of Jesus. The story does not seem to have been preserved for biographical reasons, but rather because of its contribution to kerygma, apologetics, and didactic history. It points out the Christian mission to the gentiles. Through their faith the gentiles participate in the blessings Jesus brought.

St. Mark gives us here the Pauline concept of the divine economy of salvation in story form: The Gospel is "the power of God for the salvation of everyone who believes: for Jew first, and then Greek" (Romans 1:16).

Jesus seeks privacy in Mark 7:24, possibly to reflect upon the scope of his ministry.

The Canaanite woman comes to him and prostrates herself before him.

Mark tells us that she was a Greek by religion and a Syrophoenician by race. She asks Jesus to cast a devil out of her daughter.

It is thought by some readers that Jesus treated the woman harshly here: "He said to her, 'Let the children be fed first. For it is not right to take the food of the children and throw it to the dogs'" (Mark 7:27). The word describing little dogs, puppies, and the fact that the woman makes a witty reply, seem to indicate the mildness. In short, Jesus did not call her a dog.

Our Lord seems pleased by the woman's wit and persistence and bids her depart, assuring her that the demon has gone out of her daughter. No word or promise of healing is spoken, only the assurance that the demon has gone.

"When the woman went home, she found the child lying in bed and the demon gone" (Mark 7:30).

The Boy with a Demon (Mark 9:14–29)

This miracle story abounds with detail: including the fact that the father had brought the child to three disciples who could not heal him, and the arrival of Jesus and probably the disciples.

Some think these passages are a combination of two miracle stories. The disciples play a role in verses 14–19 and then disappear; the father is the principal character in verses 21–27. The sickness is described twice. The people on hand in verse 14 also stream forward in verse 25 apparently for the first time. Mark portrays Jesus exorcising the demon as a large crowd rapidly gathered. If the story is a unit, the crowd gathering in verse 24 may be different from that in verse 14. Verses 28–29 seem to be an appendix unless they originally belonged with verses 14–19.

Moreover, a spirit is mentioned in verse 17; an unclean spirit both deaf and nonspeaking is observed in verse 25, and there are two references to foaming (verses 18 and 20).

The narratives probably have been combined, and the miracle story, strictly speaking, is verses 20–27, which lost its original conclusion, and which was imaginatively reproduced in Luke 9:43 where he describes the astonishment of the people at "the majesty of God."

In Mark 7:16–18 there is a dialogue between Jesus and a boy's father in which the boy's symptoms are described: the spirit takes hold of him and throws him down, and the son foams at the mouth, grinds his teeth, and wastes away or is completely exhausted.

The father explains that he had asked the disciples to cast out the demon, but they were not able to do so. The reference to the unbelieving generation in verse 19 probably indicates surprise at the lack of faith among people with whom Jesus had come into contact. Faith and prayer can certainly aid anyone.

A second conversation with the father begins. Jesus asks how long the boy has been afflicted. The father explained that the spirit often cast him into the fire and into the water, to destroy him.

All this leads to a most memorable exchange—for the benefit of the people present, for the disciples, and for us.

"If you can do anything," the father says to Jesus, "help us."

"All things," Jesus says, "are possible to him who believes."

The father cries out: "I believe; help my unbelief."

The statements about the exorcisms in Mark 1:32–34; 3:11–12, 15; and 6:7, 13 clearly illustrate the power of Jesus over the devil. The kingdom of God is advancing, and the kingdom of Satan is being pushed back.

IN THE VILLAGES THE SICK WERE BROUGHT UNTO HIM

CHAPTER 5

THE SIGNIFICANCE OF THE EXORCISMS

Jesus constantly was confronted with satanic power in people.

He does not say, "Bring me your possessed." Yet they come, these living manifestations of Satan on earth.

Jesus exorcises and thereby shows his power. Through these exorcisms, Jesus overcomes the kingdom of Satan: the very point he wants people to grasp.

Besides several general references, the Gospels narrate some instances in greater detail. What was the significance?

Early Christian advocates used the exorcisms as one of the arguments for the divinity of Christ. Bishop Melito of Sardis, writing in the second century about the deeds that Christ had performed, emphasized that his miracles conclusively prove that underneath the flesh was hidden the divinity.

The apologists would show that Jesus claimed to be

the Messiah and the Son of God and proved his claims by his prophecies, his miracles, his exorcisms, and especially his resurrection.

This approach still is used in current arguments. The divinity of Christ is something to be proved. Jesus Christ authenticated his claims by miracles. And since God alone is the principal cause of any genuine miracle, and he would never miraculously seal a false teaching, it follows that Jesus's claims are true: he is God.

Nineteenth century rationalists disbelieved such things as miracles. Then came the liberals, supposing that our Lord, touched by suffering, added kind actions to the history of humanitarianism.

However, it is the very essence of the Gospel to contain miracle stories. The meaning and the form of the stories bear this out entirely. The miraculous deeds are not proofs of Jesus's character, but of his Messianic authority or his divine power.

For this reason, it is not usually said that pity or the intention to quicken faith is a motive of Jesus. And the evangelists are not conscious of the problem of the relationship of his miraculous actions to his refusal of a sign. The miracles are something apart from individual will—an *automatic functioning*.

The exorcisms for Bultmann simply represent Jesus as a mighty wonder-worker. According to Martin Dibelius, the exorcisms show the superiority of Jesus as a miracle worker over all other miracle workers, saviors, and demigods.

However, that Jesus performed these exorcisms primarily out of compassion for people seems to be demonstrable. Vincent Taylor inferred that the miracle stories were told because they illustrated the power and beneficent activity of Jesus. The view is supported by Acts 10:38: "He went about doing good and healing all those oppressed by the devil; for God was with him."

"Even in the fourth Gospel (John)," noted Taylor, "the suggestion is that the 'witness' is the result of the 'works' rather than their controlling purpose" (Vincent Taylor, *The Forming of the Gospel Tradition* [London: Macmillan, 1957]).

The Gospel of Mark cites the exorcisms to show Jesus's power over Satan. Possession was a manifestation of Satan. Jesus recognizes this confrontation with Satan and reacts by casting him out.

The Gospels describe the public ministry of Jesus as one of announcing the coming of the kingdom of God. If one examines the synoptic sayings of Jesus about the exorcisms, it is clear that Jesus regarded them as signs of the inbreak of the kingdom of God. (Edwyn Hoskins and Noel Davey, *The Riddle of the New Testament* [London: Faber and Faber, 1931]). This very likely was their significance in Jesus's public ministry.

The Beelzebul controversy plainly teaches that the exorcisms are the miracles of the kingdom of God. According to all three synoptists, Jesus was accused of casting out demons in the name of the prince of the demons. Jesus replies that the power of evil cannot be divided against itself, since every kingdom so divided inevitably collapses.

Jesus already is toppling the kingdom of Satan. From one end of his ministry to the other, Jesus's constant message was the announcement of the coming of God's kingdom on earth. Moreover, he charged his disciples to preach the kingdom of God.

What, though, did he mean by the kingdom? The expelling of demons was not primarily a guarantee of the coming of the kingdom. It was one of the means by which the kingdom came on earth. (Raymond Brown, "The Gospel Miracles," *The Bible in Current Catholic Thought* [New York: Herder & Herder, 1962]).

The exorcisms were an invasion of the kingdom of Satan and a means of replacing Satan's kingdom with God's kingdom.

"The establishment of the kingdom of God," wrote Joseph Bonsirven, "had to face resistance and overt opposition from Satan. This character occupies an important place in the discourses of Jesus.

"This hostility of the adversary shows itself at the outset. In his first temptation he tries to turn the Son of God from the spiritual messianic plan. People possessed by devils realize that a decisive contest has been joined between the two powers. It is the devil who comes and sows weeds among the wheat. It is the devil who is to be the instigator of the passion of Jesus. He who comes to establish the kingdom must therefore fight against Satan. The casting out of devils is part of his mission. His constant success with unclean spirits is proof that the kingdom of God has come (Matthew 12:28)."

In short, the exorcisms by Jesus were one of the weapons to overcome Satan.

The temptation (Matthew 4:1–11, Luke 4:1–13) was placed at the beginning of Jesus's public ministry to tell us that the coming of the kingdom involved a fierce struggle between Jesus and Satan. With the sin of Adam, Satan had established his kingdom on earth. He had a certain dominion over nature and man. He would not give up his dominion without a struggle: a struggle which culminated on Calvary.

As his earthly ministry drew to a close, our Lord said, "Behold, I cast out devils and perform cures today and tomorrow, and the third day I am to end my course" (Luke 13:32).

The expelling of demons was the sign of the coming of God's kingdom: "But if it is by the Spirit of God that I drive out demons, then the kingdom of God has come upon you" (Matthew 12:28).

CHAPTER 6

THE KINGDOM OF GOD

What did the phrase "kingdom of God" or "kingdom of heaven" mean to Jesus and the Jews?

There were many connotations. The downtrodden Jews not only knew what was meant by "kingdom of God" but also expected it imminently. Through Jewish history, the phrase denoted two different ideas or hopes, at times confused and combined.

The basic meaning of the phrase "kingdom of God" is sovereignty of God, rather than sphere or realm in which God rules. The latter meaning, however, is implied.

In the Hebrew bible, the expression "kingdom of God" occurs in Wisdom 10:10 ("she … showed him the kingdom of God and gave him knowledge of holy things"), and its equivalent, the "kingdom of Yahweh" and "my kingdom" and "his kingdom" is found approximately eleven times. In all these the Hebrew and Aramaic words for kingdom have, as their primary meaning, the idea of sovereignty or kingly rule.

In the New Testament, the terms "kingdom of God"

and "kingdom of heaven" occur very frequently in the synoptics and mean the same thing. The Greek word for kingdom is *basileia*. The primary meaning is "kingship" or "rule" though it also includes the idea of realm or territory governed by a king.

The Davidic Hope of a Kingdom

In the early period of Israelite history, the kingship of Yahweh over Israel was regarded as something similar to human kingship. Each god, it was believed, ruled over his own people, to help them against their enemies and counsel them via oracles and soothsayers.

His people and his kingdom were as necessary to him as he was to them, since a God without a kingdom and a people over which to rule was inconceivable.

In the case of Israel, the sovereignty of Yahweh was absolute. Exodus 20:1–5 reads:

> I am the LORD your God, who brought you out of the land of Egypt, out of the house of slavery. You shall not have other gods beside me. You shall not make for yourself an idol or a likeness of anything in the heavens above or on the earth below or in the waters beneath the earth; you shall not bow down before them or serve them.

The kingdom of David was the kingdom of God in miniature. In David's reign, Israel's enemies were beaten, and the twelve tribes were united into one people. The

Philistines, the Moabites, the Syrians, David conquered them. Israel stood at the very zenith of its power.

In David's old age, God told him that "when your days have been completed and you rest with your ancestors, I will raise up your offspring after you, sprung from your loins, and I will establish his kingdom. He it is who shall build a house for my name, and I will establish his royal throne forever" (2 Samuel 7:12–13).

This was the notion of the kingdom of God from the time of David—the memory of a powerful kingdom and the promise of a son whose throne would be eternal and whose kingdom would be forever. In 2 Samuel 8:1–18 we read of David's wars: "The Lord brought David victory in all his undertakings."

The Jews of old, in general, did not think of the kingdom of God as a supramundane one. Rather, it was to be an earthly, political kingdom. David was an earthly king, and he would have a son, and his son would be a king, greater than David. It was to be a kingdom of this earth. And as David had been anointed, and Saul before him, so also this son of David would be anointed when he became king. Thus, he would be the anointed one.

The relationships between the word "anointed" and "Messiah" and Christ" are well known. The son of David would be a king, anointed; he would be the Messiah, the Christ. In this context there was nothing supernatural about such a title.

Furthermore, this was to be a kingdom for the Jews. It was not to be for everyone. If anyone else wanted to share in the blessings of the kingdom, he had to become a Jew first. Hence, the earliest hope of a kingdom of God was an earthly, political, and geographic kingdom.

This Davidic hope of the kingdom of God culminated in the postexilic period. On their return to Israel, the Jews thought again of the promises made by God in the past. Many saw in the person of Zorobabel the promised son of David.

The books of Haggai and Zachariah allude to the hope that great things were about to happen, per an oracle: "Now be strong, Zerubbabel ... be strong, Joshua ... be strong, all you people of the land and work! ... For I am with you ... my spirit remains in your midst; do not fear!" (Haggai 2:4–9, 21–22). "I return to Jerusalem in mercy; my house will be rebuilt there. My cities will again overflow with prosperity; the Lord will again comfort Zion and will again choose Jerusalem" (Zachariah 1:14–17). But the hoped-for kingdom never appeared.

The Danielic Hope of a Kingdom

In the same postexilic period, for the first time there was heard the theme of a new earth and new heavens. Isaiah 65:17 reads: "See, I am creating new heavens and a new earth." A new hope of the kingdom of God began to take shape. The old hope of a political, earthly kingdom did not fade away altogether but was kept alive into and beyond the times of Jesus.

The book of Daniel gave expression to a new hope. In Daniel the "kingdom" comes from heaven. The resurrection of a part of mankind will precede the establishment of this heavenly rule. Whereas the prophets of the eighth to the fifth centuries before Jesus spoke of an earthly kingdom, the dream now was of a heavenly kingdom. The universe would be transformed. All this contributed to a sharp distinction between "this age" and "the coming age." The kingdom is to be everlasting and eternal, peopled by every nation, headed by a transcendent figure like unto the son of man.

Here, then, we find two ideas. One is an earthly kingdom, headed by an earthly figure—a kingdom in which the Jewish people will be kings of the earth. The other is a heavenly kingdom, headed by a heavenly figure "like unto the son of man"—a universal kingdom. These two hopes, to be sure, were confused and combined down through Jewish history. De facto they were not quite as separate as presented here.

Jesus's Proclamation of the Kingdom of God

In the synoptic Gospels, the crowds, the disciples included, seemed to have thought of Jesus in terms of an earthly kingdom. James and John, for example, asked Christ that "we may sit one at your right and the other at your left" (Mark 10:35–37). On Palm Sunday, people cried: "Blessed is the kingdom of our father David that is to come! Hosanna in the highest!" (Mark 11:10). The people were hoping that perhaps Jesus would restore the Jewish political kingdom. They were a subject people, and now they saw Jesus. He was a man of God. He performed marvels: "Go and tell John what you have seen and heard: the blind regain their sight, the lame walk, lepers are cleansed, the deaf hear, the dead are raised, the poor have the good news proclaimed to them" (Luke 7:22). Surely, it was thought Jesus was the one to restore the earthly political kingdom.

The people literally came after Jesus in John 6:15 to force him to be their king: "Since Jesus knew that they were going to come and carry him off to make him king, he withdrew again to the mountain alone."

And what did the disciples say on the road to Emmaus: "We were hoping that he would be the one to redeem Israel" (Luke 24:21).

A careful study indicates that the people at large were looking for a kingdom of this earth like the reign of David of old. What, though, did Jesus mean by "kingdom of God?"

Jesus did not identify himself with the Davidic hope.

He was the heavenly figure of the book of Daniel, who was "like unto the son of man." This seems to be the point of Matthew 22:41–45: "What is your opinion about the Messiah? Whose son is he?" They replied, "David's." He said, "How, then, does David, inspired by the Spirit, call him 'lord,' saying: 'The Lord said to my lord, "Sit at my right hand until I place your enemies under your feet"'? If David calls him "lord," how can he be his son?"

The Jews were looking for exactly what those words say: a human son of David who would rule an earthly, political kingdom. Our Lord reminds these people that David himself saw the coming one as Lord. Jesus accepts the idea of the Messiah but rejects all its political overtones. This is why he accepted the term Christ; He was the Christ. And this perhaps is why he demanded secrecy from those who knew he was the Christ—because he rejected the ideas the term evoked.

James Kallas wrote: "In three key areas—who shall head the kingdom, the Christ or the son of man; what kind of a kingdom shall it be, earthly or celestial; who shall be its citizens, mortal Jews or resurrected representatives from all nations—in all three of these key areas we see Jesus unmistakably ally himself with the Danielic hope."

This hope of a heavenly kingdom, over which one like unto the son of man would rule, rested upon a belief that there had been a war in heaven. Satan had revolted against God and had been expelled. Now an enemy of God and no longer a servant, he tries to enslave man. It also rested on two other beliefs:

—That this earth is in Satan's kingdom. All the evils of earth, for example, famines and plagues and diseases and wars, are the doing of Satan.

—That the kingdom of Satan will be destroyed and the kingdom of God reestablished.

The hope of a kingdom of God was born of the belief that this earth was not what it should be. Death, sin, sickness, and Satan were part and parcel of the lot of man, and out of this was born the hope for the end of that earth: for a new heaven and a new earth.

Exorcisms in the Teaching of Jesus

Jesus's message was an announcement of the kingdom of God. His words and His miracles center on the kingdom of God. The kingdom of God will be the overthrowing of the kingdom of Satan. Thus, the expelling of demons is a sign of the coming of God's kingdom. At times he announced that the kingdom was coming, and at other times he spoke as if it already had come. He showed this by casting out devils.

Christ became man to bring in the kingdom of God and drive out the kingdom of Satan. Thus, the demons ask repeatedly: "What have you to do with us, Jesus of Nazareth? Have you come to destroy us? I know who you are—the Holy One of God!" (Mark 1:24).

The expelling of demons, the smashing of Satan's kingdom was proof that the kingdom of God was at hand. This is precisely what Jesus says in Matthew 12:28: "But if it is by the Spirit of God that I drive out demons, then the kingdom of God has come upon you."

Satan ruled the earth. It was his through sin. The kingdom of God advances to the extent that the time of Satan is destroyed. This happens directly through exorcisms and indirectly through the cure of diseases. God's kingdom is established by the driving out of demons and the healing of diseases. This is why the command to go and preach the kingdom of God is never separated from the command to heal and cast out demons.

The Gospels make it clear: "He summoned the twelve and began to send them out two by two and gave them authority over unclean spirits.

So they went off and preached repentance. They drove out many demons, and anointed with oil many who were sick and cured them" (Mark 6:7, 12–13).

For Jesus the healings and exorcisms were in themselves the message. They showed that the kingdom of Satan manifested in sin and sickness and death was being destroyed. This is the meaning of the kingdom of God.

This is why our Lord equates the advance of the kingdom with exorcisms and cures.

The public ministry of Jesus was the beginning of the end for Satan. In chapter 1 of the Gospel of Mark, for example, Jesus preaches the kingdom of God (Mark 1:14–15). In Mark 1:25–26 the battle lines are drawn in this kingdom of God versus kingdom of Satan conflict. The enemy is the devil. The demons see in Jesus the one who has come to destroy Satan's kingdom: "Have you come to destroy us? I know who you are—the Holy One of God!"

In Mark 1:32–34 all who were sick or possessed by demons were gathered at the door of Peter's mother-in-law. In Mark 1:39 more devils are cast out.

In Mark 3:22 the Beelzebul passage states that the expelling of demons means the overthrowing of the kingdom of Satan and the arrival of the kingdom of God. In Mark 4 there is the calming of the storm on the lake; Christ rebukes the storm as he would the devil. In Mark 5 there is the Gerasene demoniac.

For Jesus, the kingdom of God meant the overthrow of the kingdom of Satan—Satan who ruled the earth through sin and sickness and death. The exorcisms are the inbreak of the kingdom of God, the routing of the forces of evil that rule the earth. This is likely why in Mark they make up a large part of the narrative. It is the message of Jesus, pure and simple: the kingdom of God is overthrowing the kingdom of Satan.

The public ministry of Jesus was the announcement of the actual commencement of that destruction. Christ manifested His power over Satan. The climax of the destruction of Satan's kingdom occurred on the cross and at the resurrection.

If the ministry of our Lord is viewed as the defeat of Satan, then the life, work, death, and resurrection of Jesus become a unified whole. He begins his fight with Satan in the exorcisms and cures, attacks Satan where he is strongest by bringing people back to life, and then triumphs himself over death.

The exorcisms were one of the weapons Jesus used to overcome Satan. The expelling of demons was the infallible sign of the coming of the kingdom, showing the triumph of God's kingdom over Satan's kingdom.

Exorcisms in the Primitive Church

It is important to distinguish the various levels in the synoptic tradition in the interpretation of these exorcisms.

For Jesus, the exorcisms announced the coming of the kingdom of God. They were signs of the messianic age.

The primitive church reinterpreted these exorcisms as signs that Jesus was the Messiah. The exorcisms are signs that Jesus is "He who is to come" (Matthew 11:3). "And Jesus answering said to them, 'Go and report to John what you have heard and seen: the blind see, the lame walk, the lepers are cleansed, the deaf hear, the dead rise, the poor have the gospel preached to them'" (Matthew 11:4–5).

The demoniac in the synagogue, for example, says, "Have you come to destroy us? I know who thou art, the Holy One of God." The Holy One of God is a messianic title. The demon perceives Christ to be the Messiah.

In the story of the Gerasene demoniac, the demon

cries out, "What have you to do with us, Jesus of Nazareth?" Jesus is identified with the Messiah.

In the story of the Syrophoenician woman, Reginald Fuller points out that "Jesus is the giver of the Messianic bread. This bread was intended first for the children of Israel; but the dogs (that is, the gentiles) may participate in the messianic salvation, although this privilege comes through faith alone. We can see the early Church wrestling here with the problem of the gentile mission."

The exorcism of the boy with epilepsy is an illustration of faith. "Faith," writes Fuller, "on one side and the act of God on the other are between them able to do all things, even overcome the power of evil."

Part of the messianic blessing of the kingdom of God will be the overcoming of this evil. Thus for the primitive church the exorcisms are more than signs of the coming of the kingdom of God and the overthrow of the kingdom of Satan. The early church interpreted these as signs that Jesus was the Messiah. Christ for the church releases humankind from the bondage of Satan and gives them the blessings of his salvation.

E. Hoskyns wrote of the miracles in the Gospel of St. Mark: "The Marcan miracle narratives which at first sight seem to record conventional actions of a wonder-worker are found upon closer investigation to have a wholly different significance. The Marcan miracles are signs that the Messiah is present in the heart of Judaism and signs warranted by Old Testament prophecy. Moreover, they are not only signs of His presence, they are signs of the nature of His power since they point away from mere physical healing to freedom from sin and to the recognition of the power of the Living God" (E. Hoskyns, *Cambridge Sermons*).

Finally, there is Mark's interpretation of the exorcisms. Fuller summarizes this well in interpreting the miracles, so I will briefly outline the substance of his views.

Fuller studies the arrangement and ordering of the miracles, and postulates that there are five groups in Mark's Gospel.

The first series is found in Mark 1:1–39. Fuller sees two ideas in the series. Jesus is in conflict with His human enemies in His teaching, and He is in conflict with the demons and with sickness in his miracles.

In the second group (Mark 1:40 to 3:6) Fuller thinks Mark is telling readers that Jesus's conflicts with human enemies are part of a conflict which is to culminate with His passion and death and resurrection.

The third group (Mark 3:7–30) consists of a summary of exorcism and prepares the way for the Beelzebub controversy. Mark spells out clearly that the exorcisms are the struggle between the spirit of God and the powers of evil.

In the fourth group (Mark 4:35, 5:43) Jesus is in conflict with his disciples and the conflict is not resolved until Peter confesses at Caesarea Philippi, "You are the Christ" (Mark 8:29).

In the fifth group of miracles (Mark 6:30, 8:26) Jesus's struggle with the misunderstanding of the disciples continues.

This, in short, is the significance of the exorcisms on the three levels of the Gospels.

For Jesus, the exorcisms announced the inbreak of the kingdom of God.

For the primitive church, the exorcisms are signs that Jesus was the Messiah.

Finally, for Mark, the exorcisms are signs of Jesus's conflict with His enemies and His disciples.

CHAPTER 7

INCLUDING THE EXORCISMS
IN FAITH FORMATION

There have been various methods of teaching about exorcisms (manifestations of Satan). Here are highlights of representative samples from two illustrious religious educators, Vincent Novak and Johannes Hofinger, and some suggestions on presenting the exorcisms more fruitfully in catechesis.

In *Jesus Christ Lord of History*, Vincent Novak does not treat exorcisms per se. He does bring out now and then the kingdom of God/kingdom of Satan conflict.

For example, Novak explains how the combat between Satan and Jesus broke out in the temptation in the desert. Jesus won the skirmish but not the war. This struggle will continue to Christ's final triumph on Judgment Day. Humankind may choose to serve beneath Satan's flag or rally around the standard of Christ.

In chapter 12 of *Jesus Christ Lord of History* Novak illustrates how Jesus made use of miracles. The purpose varies. Some were intended to show God's goodness and mercy, others to encourage the apostles and support Jesus's Messianic mission, and still others to teach spiritual truths through visible signs, or to give a preview of life after death.

Novak highlights the final clash between Jesus and Satan in the arrest of Jesus. Satan takes over: he whipped up evil spirits in men in order to take revenge upon this Messiah who would take away the sins of the world. Christ, however, triumphs on Easter Sunday. He returns to the Father and will come again in glory. On that day the final destiny of humankind will be sealed. Satan will be crushed; his kingdom will lay in ruins.

Novak alludes to the exorcisms in his second book, *Jesus Christ Our Life and Worship*. The prayers of exorcism in the rite of baptism purify the candidate of the devil's influence.

Johannes Hofinger's *The Art of Teaching Christian Doctrine* refers to Satan. Our first parents were tempted by the devil; deceived by him, they sinned grievously, knowingly, and freely. They transgressed a serious command of God; they rebelled and thereby established the kingdom of Satan on earth. God in his mercy promised a savior; the Son of God will become the son of man to make us sons and daughters of God, coheirs of the kingdom of God.

Hofinger brings out in his instruction on baptisms how they indicate that Christ is driving out the former owner, who has stolen us from our Creator, but the devil does not relinquish his hold on us unless we ourselves wish it.

The climax of baptism has traditionally been a personal renouncement of the devil: "I do renounce him."

Finally, there is the *Catechism of the Council of Trent for Parish Priests*. It alludes to the exorcisms in its lesson on baptism and on temptation. However, this treatment is not detailed.

Manifestations of Satan in Salvation History

Most people today, if they think of Satan at all, size him up as somebody like themselves: a bundle of strengths and weaknesses, knowledge and ignorance, successes and failures. When Satan does cross their minds, he's way off somewhere comfortably distant from themselves, so they think he isn't there.

The attitude of the Jews in biblical times was much healthier, if less attractive. Satan was regarded as the ultimate source of all evil. The Bible calls him "the evil one." It was Satan who had caused Adam to sin, and Satan who has had a hand in every sin committed since then. The penalties of Adam's sin—moral weakness, ignorance, suffering, and death—were also Satan's handiwork. And because these things were and still are found in such abundance, the Jews were always conscious of Satan's presence in one form or another.

Probably the best way to present the exorcism manifestations of Satan is in the context of salvation history.

The Bible introduces us to the kingdom of Satan: sin, sickness and death were established on earth. The kingdom of God/kingdom of Satan conflict, which continues down until the end of time, began here. Genesis 3:15 speaks of God's ultimate victory over Satan: "I will put enmity between you and the woman, and between your offspring and hers; they will strike at your head, while you strike at their heel."

Man is falling into the hands of Satan, and God has promised deliverance. The next eight chapters show the ruthlessness with which Satan invades the earth. Against this backdrop of sin, sickness, death, and Satan, Genesis introduces us to Abraham: the father of the chosen people. Humankind has fallen further and further away from God—is giving in to Satan more and more—and then God dramatically steps in.

In the twelfth chapter of Genesis, God chooses Abraham as the vessel of salvation; in him all the nations of the earth will be blessed. Through his offspring, the kingdom of Satan will be overthrown and the kingdom of God reestablished on earth.

The catechist can show in wonderful ways how in the beginning God made the heavens and the earth, how in poetic words:

> He said, Bring forth! Bring forth!
> And quicker than God could drop his hand,
> fishes and fowls
> and beasts and birds
> swam the rivers and the seas,
> roamed the forests and the woods,
> and split the air with their wings.
> And God said: That's good!

This vision by James Weldon Johnson ("The Creation" in *God's Trombones*. Viking Press, 1927), the first African-American professor at New York University and a well-known attorney during the Harlem Renaissance, brings a tremendous insight: everything mirrors some perfection of God's. This material universe—earth and sea and sky—all was born of God and was good, for when God gave this earth its beginning, he was painting his own features on the canvas of the world: a mountain mirrors his majesty and a star-flecked sky his breathtaking loveliness.

And yet God was still not fully satisfied with his masterpiece. And so "God created mankind in his image; in the image of God he created them; male and female he created them" (Genesis 1:27).

It is vitally important that the catechist point up the goodness of creation and contrast it sharply against the wickedness of Satan. The paradise God created in Genesis shows us the first man and the first woman and the first sin. For the man and the woman, whom God had made to father and mother the human race and pass on to their children for all time the life and love of God, had sinned.

The catechist can bring out how Satan attacked God's plan of love for humankind and poisoned humanity at its source. People will be lured from God by the devil beneath them, by the devil about them, and by the devil within them.

But there is one thing stronger than sin, and that is love. In the third chapter of Genesis, God doomed Satan to defeat. "Then the LORD God said to the snake: Because you have done this, cursed are you among all the animals" (Genesis 3:14).

God told the devil he will raise up a new man and a new woman, and a barrier of grace.

Genesis tells us that creation was a good thing. Then came Satan and his kingdom. Chapters 4 to 11 show how that kingdom grows: sin, death, and sickness. In chapter 12 God intervenes and chooses Abraham as his vessel of salvation. The covenant made with Abraham was renewed with Isaac and Jacob and Joseph.

When Jewish fortunes in Egypt seem to have reached their lowest depth, when God's plan of salvation seemed to have been ruined, when Satan seemed to have doomed God, a deliverer was sent to the Jews. God decisively intervened in history in the person of Moses.

The next three hundred years were an age of migration under Moses, conquest under Joshua, confederation under the judges, and the rise of the monarchy under Saul, David, and Solomon. Once again, the kingdom of God seemed to have gotten the upper hand; once again Satan seemed doomed.

Of the first three kings, David was the most extraordinary. Through the passage of time he remained the king of Israel. His role in the eventual overthrow of the kingdom of Satan was most important.

David and his descendants entered in a special way into God's plan. His kingdom was to be an eternal one, and in a way and at a time unknown to him, universal. The birth of every Davidic prince, the consecration of every Davidic king in future years was to be an occasion of rejoicing, for that prince, that king, would stand close to God and perhaps would be the Messiah. This Messiah would do battle with Satan and defeat him. With David, therefore, God's plan of salvation takes another significant step forward. From this time on the hopes of Israel and indeed the hopes of the world were directed toward the Davidic dynasty, toward the king reigning at that moment, and toward the great king who was to come. In this way, the kingdom of God would be reestablished on earth and the kingdom of Satan overthrown once and for all.

The history of Israel from Solomon to the exile was a time of decline. It began with the division of the kingdom after Solomon's death, continued through the Assyrian destruction of the northern kingdom, and culminated in the fall of Jerusalem and the Babylonian exile of 587 BC.

Satan and sin seemed to be engulfing more and more of the earth. The prophets with God's help were able to offset Satan to an extent.

Amos and others are among the few whose stories have come down to us. They addressed their message of doom to the corrupt political and religious leaders who through their sins were spreading the kingdom of Satan. These prophets told them that the day of the Lord would be one of invasion, destruction, and fire and sword unless they repented.

The prophets spoke out so forcefully because they saw more than anyone else the manifestations of the kingdom of Satan: namely sin.

The catechist can also bring out how the prophets foresaw the survival of a "remnant" and the intervention of God in history to establish the kingdom of God forever.

The final period of Israel's pre-Christian history includes the fifty years of exile and the five centuries of attempted restoration, when the hope for religious and political revival became intense. Two scripture passages are especially noteworthy in this.

The first are the servant songs in Deutero-Isaiah: Isaiah 42:17, 49:1–6, 50:4–9, 52:13, 53:12. These poems describe Israel as God's servant, an individual who represents the nation and who undergoes suffering not only for Israel but for all nations.

The other passage is the description of the Son of Man in Daniel 7. In this vision of the end, the great world powers are represented by four animals: like a lion with eagle's wings, a bear, a leopard, and "a fourth beast, terrifying, horrible, and of extraordinary strength." In a divine judgment, power is taken from these kingdoms and transferred to "one like unto a Son of Man," that is, an individual in human form. This individual represents "the saints of the Most High"—Israel.

The vision then represents the promise of an everlasting and universal kingdom to be transferred by God to Israel represented by an individual known in Jewish tradition as the Son of Man.

The catechist here can point out the deep significance of this vision. The kingdom of God will triumph over the kingdom of Satan and will triumph over sin and sickness and death. With the coming of Jesus into the world, a direct attack was made on the kingdom of Satan.

Jesus attacks the manifestations of the kingdom of Satan—sin, sickness, death—and shows his power over them. He cures a leper, a centurion's servant, Peter's mother-in-law, a paralytic at Capernaum, a woman with a hemorrhage. He restores sight to the blind, casts out

Satan from demoniacs, brings back to life the daughter of a synagogue official, and forgives the sins of a paralytic.

Jesus unmistakably shows his power over every characteristic of Satan's kingdom. The kingdom of Satan is beginning to collapse, and the kingdom of God is being reestablished on earth.

Christ's community of disciples—the church—has power over Satan with the apostles. They begin to cure demoniacs and heal the sick.

But the battle between Jesus and Satan, so evident throughout Jesus's public ministry, culminated on Calvary. This was the hour that the world had been waiting for since the fall of our first parents: the hour at which the kingdom of Satan would give way to the kingdom of God. Satan's chief characteristics were sin and death. The Crucifixion scored the victory over sin; the resurrection conquered death. Christ broke death's power over humankind.

Salvation consisted precisely in Jesus's Crucifixion and resurrection from the dead. In reconciling us with God and in overcoming death, the kingdom of God overthrew the kingdom of Satan.

Baptismal Exorcisms

Although Christ triumphed over Satan on Easter, this does not mean that human beings personally share in this victory. The catechist must show, how does one personally overcome the kingdom of Satan?

This is done fundamentally through faith and the sacraments and through love; through these we share in Christ's victory. Through the sacraments especially, human beings conquer Satan.

Baptism spotlights the victory of Christ. We enter as sinners and emerge graced. We enter as subjects of death and the devil and emerge as beloved sons and daughters of God. Yes, in baptism we pass over from the kingdom of Satan to the kingdom of God. This marks the beginning of our lifelong battle against Satan.

Hence an essential part of the rite of baptism is the

renunciation of Satan. An exorcism prayer is recited over the person being baptized. The intention is for the person to renounce sin and Satan—his works, his temptations. Parents, godparents, and the entire community do this on behalf of an infant who cannot yet speak for himself or herself.

The renunciation of Satan and commitment to Christ is no easy thing, and so the church, the community of disciples, prepares for this by reminding us that "the whole world is under the power of the evil one" (1 John 5:19).

The baptismal exorcisms consist of prayers, commands, and gestures. The chief of these is the sign of the cross, which the priest makes with his thumb on the person being baptized, saying, "Receive the mark of the cross on your forehead and within your heart. Embrace the faith with its divine teachings. So live that you will indeed be a temple of God."

In past versions of the rite, immediately before the sign of the cross, the priest blew gently three times on the face of the infant (as if blowing away the devil) and said, "Depart from him, unclean spirit, and give place to the Holy Spirit the consoler."

Christ triumphed over Satan, sin, sickness, and death on the cross, and in the resurrection the sign of the cross points to the victory of the kingdom of God over the kingdom of Satan.

The baptismal rite retains a number of references to this conflict within humans. The reception into the church symbolizes the leaving of the realm of Satan and the entering into the kingdom of God. The catechist should bring out the significance of these formulae in the presentation of the exorcisms.

The passion, death, and resurrection of Christ definitely spelled the defeat of Satan's kingdom with regard to death.

The earthly life of a Christian, though, is still a warfare. Throughout life, one has to fight against Satan's works and temptations. Only at the Parousia will Christ decisively destroy the last vestiges of Satan's kingdom.

This idea is brought out in the baptismal rite when the celebrant puts on the candidate a white garment or linen cloth upon the head, as a reminder of Christ's protective love and an admonition to keep the garment unstained by sin: "They have washed their robes and made them white in the blood of the Lamb" (Revelation 7:14). The white garment is the Christian sign of victory over Satan.

The Parousia idea is also evident when the priest gives the baptized a lighted candle, reminding the newly baptized of the light of Christ that all those baptized are to be for the world.

The symbols of the white cloth and candle appear again in the Roman Catholic funeral liturgy.

Hence if baptism means a battle, it also means a victory. If it means renouncement of Satan, it also means a commitment to Christ.

To be baptized is to become one with Christ. It is a new birth, a new life. It is the very life of God. We are incorporated into the kingdom of God and thereby share in Christ's victory over Satan.

The Anointing of the Sick

The catechist can bring out the kingdom of God/kingdom of Satan conflict in the anointing of the sick.

Sickness is a characteristic of the kingdom of Satan, and Jesus treated it as such in his public ministry. The sick came to him, and he cured them.

In this way Jesus initiated—and through the anointing of the sick he carries on—the struggle against Satan, and sin and sickness and death are a struggle that is to culminate in the triumph of God's kingdom over Satan's.

In the present rite, the priest anoints the forehead and says, "Through this holy anointing, may the Lord in his love and mercy help you with the grace of the Holy Spirit."

Then he anoints the hands and clearly says, "May the Lord who frees you from sin save you and raise you up."

Exorcisms in the Sacramental Life of the Church

Baptism enables the Christian to renounce Satan day by day.

The Eucharist strengthens the Christian in this struggle.

The rite of reconciliation not only liberates a Christian from Satan's kingdom but also strengthens him in the fight against temptation.

The anointing of the sick helps the Christian struggle against temptation in the wake of sickness.

Confirmation enables us to become witnesses to Christ: "You will receive power when the holy Spirit comes upon you, and you will be my witnesses in Jerusalem, throughout

Judea and Samaria, and to the ends of the earth" (Acts 1:8). Yes, we carry the kingdom of God worldwide.

The Christian experiences salvation in the church—the community of disciples of Jesus. This salvation involves not only the overcoming of Satan's kingdom but also a sharing in the very life of God: a life that our first parents lost through their sin of pride and disobedience. Further sin drove us further and further from God.

With Abraham, humankind started on the way back to God.

When Jesus came, he overthrew Satan's kingdom and incorporated us into the kingdom of God through grace.

Eschatological Significance of the Exorcisms

The exorcisms can contrast the lot of the person committed to Christ and the lot of the person opposed to him. They teach the ultimate lot of one opposed to Christ.

The so-called last things—death, judgment, heaven and hell—are a manifestation of the age-old conflict between the kingdom of God and the kingdom of Satan. With death one's eternal destiny is fixed irrevocably. When we die, we belong irrevocably either to God or to Satan.

The Christian is reminded in the words of the Eucharistic Prayer of a Catholic Funeral Liturgy that "life is changed, not taken away; and when the home of this earthly sojourn is dissolved, an eternal dwelling is made ready in heaven."

Whenever death occurs, there is a Parousia, a manifestation of the power and glory of our Lord. It is the Christian's encounter with the living Christ.

At the time of death, our Lord comes to each person and says, "Prepare a full account of your stewardship" (Luke 16:2). Obviously, this is our complete incorporation into Christ or else is our complete exclusion. It seals us as either God's or Satan's. At the moment of death, God or Satan takes hold. On judgment day our life will appear plainly: not simply as a whole, but in every instance where we have accepted or rejected grace, in every situation where we have chosen the kingdom of God or the kingdom of Satan.

In fact, we shall encounter once again our own life and in unison with our judge record the verdict. That will be either a miserable end or a blessed beginning.

Every action or omission increases within us the dominion of God or of Satan. Christ will reject those who belong to Satan and welcome unendingly those who belong to him. Hell is death. Just as by grace we become a member of God's kingdom, so by sin we become a member of Satan's kingdom. Instead of being a manifestation of grace, one is a manifestation of Satan. This is precisely what an exorcism addresses.

Damnation means exclusion from the marriage hall, from the eternal banquet, and from the heavenly Jerusalem. It means incorporation into the kingdom of Satan.

Heaven, on the other hand, is the kingdom of God. Hence when the last things take place, they signify a phase in the great battle between Christ and Satan. And Satan is never the victor, even when sinners fall into his hands. Every battle between Satan and Christ is lost to Satan. For Christ alone is Lord of the universe and of history.

The Parousia will bring history to its fulfillment. The whole of history leads up to it. Just as from the time of Adam history advanced forward to Calvary, so from Calvary history hastens on to the ultimate manifestation of the Lord's presence and power.

The appearance of the antichrist will be a sign of the Parousia. According to 2 Thessalonians 2:3–4, he is "the one doomed to perdition, who opposes and exalts himself above every so-called god and object of worship, so as to seat himself in the temple of God, claiming that he is a god."

In 1 John 2:18 we read: "Just as you heard that the antichrist was coming, so now many antichrists have appeared. Thus we know this is the last hour." Unprecedented terrors will prelude the last day. The success of the antichrist will be tremendous. There will be apostasy on a large scale.

Then Christ will come. "I saw a large white throne and the one who was sitting on it. The earth and the sky fled from his presence and there was no place for them. I saw the dead, the great and the lowly, standing before the throne, and scrolls were opened. Then another scroll was opened, the book of life. The dead were judged according to their deeds, by what was written in the scrolls" (Revelation 20:11–12).

The last judgment will be the manifestation of Christ—of the glory and dominion of the Lamb, who, slain for the redemption of the world, continued his work through history. This judgment will be the definitive establishment of the kingdom of God. With the coming of Christ, Satan's dominion will cease altogether, and death will be no more. "Then the word that is written shall come about: 'Death is swallowed up in victory'" (1 Corinthians 15:54).

When a Christian dies the great question is: Was I a manifestation of Christ? Is the Lord who lives and acts in His church, the community of disciples, visible in me? At the Parousia, the Lord, always secretly present in the church, will make his presence visible. It will be clear what God expected of each person to further the kingdom of God, and how the person was correspondingly endowed with talents and graces.

On judgment day the separation will be made between those who were a manifestation of Christ and those who were a manifestation of Satan.

In short, the decisive question is: Do I belong to God's kingdom or Satan's?

Those who have rejected the kingdom of God will form the kingdom of Satan, and they will see the futility and meaninglessness of their lives—of all their efforts to erase God's image from His creation, when all they did was erase it from themselves.

The resurrection of the dead will be the last act of Christ's conquest of Satan. People must be raised up from corruption. The decay of the body is a characteristic of Satan's kingdom. Only when we are raised can there be a victory over death.

And finally, all things will be renewed. There will be no place in the universe for Satan. He will be expelled forever. The kingdom of God will be definitively established and the kingdom of Satan overthrown once and for all.

CHAPTER 8

KEEPING THE DEVIL AWAY

God's generous creativity gives us life, and Jesus shows us the way and truth for the fullness of life. Yes, who can forget Jesus's firm denial of distraction in Matthew 16: "Get thee behind me, Satan!"

The Holy Spirit—the same Spirit that people witnessed when Jesus was baptized—pours out gifts for each of us, so that we may manifest "love, joy, peace, patience, kindness, generosity, faithfulness, gentleness, self-control" (Galatians 5). And every action prompted by the Spirit increases the kingdom of God on earth.

Satan, on the other hand, desires to disrupt God's kingdom.

Despite God's generosity—to the point of entrusting his only begotten son to us for eternal life—we may be tempted by temporal maladies. St. Paul signposts the obvious: "immorality, impurity, licentiousness, idolatry, sorcery, hatreds, rivalry, jealousy, outbursts of fury, acts of selfishness, dissensions, factions, occasions of envy, drinking bouts, orgies, and the like."

Those maladies are a sign of Satan's desire to destroy our relationship with God. Evil—sin—is a gap between oneself and God. Think of the sign on English subway platforms: "Mind the gap."

While "no eye has seen" what heaven has in store, it would be painful to let the living God within be erased from one's consciousness and to condemn oneself to a hell on earth of anger, addictions, and the like.

Evil is contagious, or cancerous. Greed and promiscuity, for example, can lead to victimization of others. Addiction and fury can lead to violence and death. Those relationships definitely separate us from knowledge of God's care for us and limit the abundant life for which we were created.

There can be an attraction to the powerful effects of substances such as alcohol and drugs. Not the attraction of healing, which is a legitimate reason for medications, but the addiction to effects that make us less like ourselves. Less joyful, less kind, less faithful, less in control. There is certainly a difference between attraction and addiction. Yet being open to either—and being willing to disconnect human feelings—can be an invitation to evil. Better to seek a doctor's counsel early on, consult with a trusted relative/friend or pastor, and pray. God is closer to you than you are to yourself.

Many persons convicted of crimes admit they "drugged up" to remove their feelings—their human conscience—before doing the very bad things they did.

There are other addictions. The serial killer Jeffrey Dahmer began with thoughts and fantasies: "Control, power, complete dominance. There was excitement, fear, pleasure, all mixed together." Dahmer said he "didn't like feeling evil, tried to overcome the thoughts, but eventually gave in."

In his own words, Dahmer's compulsion was "addictive." His ritual was to go out, drink, go to clubs, then drug, rape, kill, and dismember victims.

Notably, he was also attracted to *The Exorcist 3* as part of his ritual. "I felt so hopelessly evil and perverted that I actually derived pleasure from that tape," he said.

In his evil acts, he felt "a surge of energy." He even planned to set up an altar with skulls/skeletons of his victims as a sort of memorial, "a place to collect my thoughts and feed the obsession." The compulsion was "the only thing that gave me any satisfaction," he said.

In short, Jeffrey Dahmer took steps that dehumanized himself and others. He was convicted of sixteen homicides. In prison, after he repented and was baptized, Dahmer was killed by a fellow inmate.

Decades later, society has begun to grapple with complex issues including personality disorders, psychosis, and possession.

People in positions of authority are not immune to temptations. A teacher, a coach, or a religious official may struggle—may have abused minors, distorting the role of sexuality, using it as a weapon instead of as a sacramental element from God. Individuals must all be vigilant of self-control and integrity, especially those charged to "practice what they preach."

The Catholic Church has certainly improved its policies and practices in the last couple of decades, in consideration of the physical, mental, and spiritual health of all its members. While an individual bears responsibility for personal behavior, it takes a truly prayerful community to practice justice and reject sin.

As the saying goes, an ounce of prevention is worth a pound of cure. In fact, AA groups, SA groups, and WW workshops have members from early stage to severe addictions to "recovering."

All of these self-help support groups use an approach of recognizing one's unhelpful thoughts, checking one's perception versus reality, and charting a better course. Several "12 step" groups embrace the Serenity Prayer, adapted from this sermon excerpt by Protestant theologian Reinhold Niebuhr:

> God, give us the grace to accept with serenity the things I cannot change; courage to change the things I can; and wisdom to know the difference. Living one day at a time; enjoying one moment at a time; accepting hardships as the pathway to peace; taking, as He did, this sinful world as it is, not as I would have it; trusting that He will make all things right if I surrender to His Will.

> (originated circa 1932, sermon 1943, published by Niebuhr's daughter Elisabeth Sifton in *The Serenity Prayer*, W.W. Norton, 2003).

St. Paul warned St. Timothy, and us, that idle minds are the devil's workshop. By not using time productively, people "learn to be idlers … gossips and busybodies as well, talking about things that ought not to be mentioned," Paul wrote (1 Timothy 5:13). In essence, their idleness was leading them into sin.

Paul also cautioned the early Christian community in Thessalonica, Greece:

> We hear that some are conducting themselves among you in a disorderly way, by not keeping busy but minding the business of others. Such people we instruct and urge in the Lord Jesus Christ to work quietly and to eat their own food. But you, brothers, do not be remiss in doing good. (2 Thessalonians 3:10–13)

Idleness often stems from not having a goal or purpose. If we have nothing to do, the devil is eager to find things to occupy our time.

Fr. Vincent Lampert, an Indianapolis priest and exorcist, finds that "Where people have heard the good news, but turned away from it, it seems evil can make a greater claim on them." But this exorcist remains prayerful and focused: "No one is ever lost to God. God can reach anyone."

Whether a believer or unbeliever, human beings share a common humanity. All of us experience some brokenness or incompleteness in our lives.

Who really are we? There are as many answers as there are people. But occasionally we may wonder. In a moment of crisis, one may not be able to answer the question, but we cannot help but answer by the way we choose to live.

Rick Warren, founding pastor of Saddleback Church in California, has an interesting book titled *What on Earth Am I Here For*, an expanded edition of *The Purpose Driven Life*. A guide in our spiritual journey, the book attempts to show answers to three of life's most important questions: Why am I alive? Does my life have purpose? What on earth am I here for?

If we know our purpose, we will simplify our life, focus on it, increase our motivation, and prepare for eternity.

Does my life matter? Do I have a purpose? There are but two possible answers.

One is no: Life is meaningless, absurd. Some philosophers of existentialist thought, for example, Sartre, Nietzsche, and Camus, speak about the absurdity of life. But ultimately, they urge us to give life meaning ourselves.

The other answer is yes. Life involves experiences; experiences involve change; and change involves movement. Movement can be directioned or directionless.

We search for a way, a means. If being human means to live in relationships, the answer will be found, not alone, but in community.

Religion attempts to answer the question of meaning. The word *religion* resembles the Latin word *religare*, or "to tie together."

Our ligaments tie our bones together. So too religion aims to make sense out of our lives—to tie things together.

Hence, religion can be defined as an explanation of the meaning of human life, grounded in the notion of God and how human beings live accordingly. Religion contains a set of beliefs or a creed, a code of behavior, ritual activities that relate us to the transcendent God and one another, and a network of human relationships. Religion, in the final analysis, is a way of living. The goal may be redemption, liberation, enlightenment, salvation, heaven.

So who are we? British theologian John Macquarrie, an authority on the philosopher Martin Heidegger and the biblical scholar Rudolf Bultmann, recognizes that we are human beings who live either with faith in God or no faith.

What differentiates us from other beings? People, cats, trees, rocks all are. But as far as we know, only human beings are aware that they are, and aware to a degree of *what* they are. Yes, human beings are conscious of their kinship with animals and nature, and at the same time they are aware of what separates them from animals and nature.

Human beings are capable, to some extent, of self-direction. Our selfhood is always incomplete at any given moment. Authentic selfhood is a potentiality to be responsibly actualized. Therefore, we can attain it or miss it. We are human beings with tensions or polarities within us. We have potential but at the same time, limitations— for example, physical size, mental aptitude, social skills, emotional maturity, and so forth.

We are rational and irrational. We observe, judge and act, and we do things without knowing why. We are responsible yet at times irresponsible. We know what we have to do, and yet sometimes we don't do it. In short, we have free will.

We are individuals and, at the same time, social; we cannot live apart from others. And then ultimately there is death. We came out of nothingness at a particular time and will fall back into nothingness at another time.

To complicate matters, human beings must find purpose in a disordered universe. There is so much evil— for example, wars, genocides, random violence. So many people seem to be alienated from one another, even from themselves.

Christianity calls this sin, a "missing the mark" relative to our relationships with one another and to ourselves. St. Augustine called it "original sin."

Theologian John Macquarrie would describe it as a failure to achieve our authentic selfhood. The nineteenth century Russian author Feodor Dostoyevsky described powerfully this so-called "alienation" in his novel *Notes from the Underground.*

Can we find purpose in life in a disordered universe?

Sartre would say no—that life is a useless passion—and the best we can do is reduce its oppressiveness.

If we still seek purpose in life, we frankly must look beyond ourselves. Christianity calls this "grace."

Yes, we struggle to make sense out of things, to create order out of chaos, and to realize our true potential. In other words, the authentic self is not ready-made but has to be made in the course of a lifetime.

What we have at the outset is the potentiality for becoming our authentic self. The self, made up of polarities or tensions, holds together the three dimensions of past, present, and future by means of a commitment to some master possibilities on the one hand and the acceptance of limitations on the other.

Death is the ultimate limiting factor. Death more than anything else brings before us our own radical finitude. We have to evaluate all our possibilities in light of death. In one sense, death is destructive; in another sense, creative. Death exposes the triviality of many of the ambitions and aspirations on which we spend our energies.

Human existence makes sense only if there is some

power beyond us to help us realize our authentic selfhood. That power is God.

Neither the person of faith nor the person of unfaith has certitude. We live in ambiguity and yet have to decide how we will live. Christianity argues that we find purpose ultimately in God, who revealed himself to us in Jesus Christ and is alive among us by the power of the spirit.

Yes, the ultimate purpose of life, from a Christian perspective, no matter who we are or what we do, is to be in relationship with God forever. How to achieve this? Through God's initiative and our response. We have to let the breath or spirit of God live, breathe, and work in us.

There are many spiritual pathways into relationship with God. In Catholic Christianity, for example, Benedictine, Franciscan, Dominican, Carmelite, Jesuit, Ursuline, priestly, and lay communities have different emphases. But they are all responses to God's one call to all of us. In other words, holiness is as diverse as are human beings.

Pope Francis, in his apostolic exhortation "Rejoice and Be Glad," highlights simply but practically what it means to be holy. The Beatitudes in the Gospels of Matthew (chapter 5) and Luke (chapter 6) are our identity card, so Pope Francis writes. Then he builds on the meaning of each beatitude.

Disciples of Jesus recognize who they are (mere creatures of an all-mighty Creator); they seek God in their daily lives; they forgive wrongs done to them; they are peacemakers, bridge-builders; and, yes, they're always ready to do the right thing. The beatitudes are indeed a splendid spiritual guide in striving for our authentic holy selfhood.

Holiness is for everyone. It is doing whatever our life's work is as best we can.

Mercy or forgiveness is the heart of the Gospel. What we do for God and others is the basis upon which our lives will be judged. Mother Teresa of Calcutta put it well when she wrote that God "depends on us to love the world and to show how much he loves it."

The Christian life is indeed a battle. We need strength and courage and grace from God to withstand the temptations of the devil. This struggle at its core is with the devil. Pope Francis makes it clear that the devil is not "a myth, a figure of speech, or an idea. The devil does not need to possess us. He simply poisons us with the venom of hatred, desolation, envy and vice."

"Rejoice and Be Glad" calls all of us to be saints. The exhortation offers many examples of holy lives, for example, Francis of Assisi, Clare of Assisi, Therese of Lisieux, Ignatius of Loyola. Doing our life's work as best we can is holiness.

The exhortation has plenty of practical advice for living a life of holiness. And the Beatitudes are a road map for holiness: "seeing and acting with mercy." And with God's grace, we will achieve our authentic self-hood, our true purpose in life.

Focus on God. As St. Francis of Assisi asked:

"Who are you, my God, and who am I?" Know that God is. We humans are not God, but God sees himself in each of us, and you may see yourself in God. Better that than Satan, who wants to remove the very "humanness" from human beings. Francis often sang praise to God. (Francis apparently never sang to Satan.)

Personal prayer is a close, two-way conversation with God. Contemplating the word of God in scripture also informs us about the amazing presence of our Creator.

And gathering in community is essential. We have the example of Jesus, as a youngster: "After three days [his parents] found him in the temple, sitting in the midst of the teachers, listening to them and asking them questions, and all who heard him were astounded at his understanding and his answers. When his parents saw him, they were astonished, and his mother said to him, 'Son, why have you done this to us? Your father and I have been looking for you with great anxiety.' And he said to them, 'Why were you looking for me? Did you not know that I must be in my Father's house?'" (Luke 2:46–49).

As a young adult, Jesus sacrificed his life for us, so that sins may be forgiven, and we have the opportunity for a new creation.

According to Pope Francis, the Eucharist provides the nourishment needed to truly live the Gospel well in our daily lives.

"How can we practice the Gospel without drawing the necessary strength to do it, one Sunday after another, from the inexhaustible spring of the Eucharist?" the pope said to a general audience. "We Christians need to participate in Sunday Mass because only with the grace of Jesus, with his living presence in us and among us, can we put into practice his commandment, and thus be his credible witnesses," he said. We go to Mass "to receive from Him what we really need."

"All one's ways are pure in one's own eyes,
but the measurer of motives is the LORD.

Entrust your works to the LORD, and your
plans will succeed." (Proverbs 16:2–3)

INDEX

Printed in the United States
By Bookmasters